# Credits

**Author**
Luca Dentella

**Reviewers**
Mark Fermin
Andy Paul
Anton van Pelt

**Commissioning Editor**
Usha Iyer

**Acquisition Editors**
Pramila Balan
Shaon Basu

**Content Development Editor**
Shaon Basu

**Technical Editors**
Ankita Jha
Sebastian Rodrigues

**Copy Editors**
Gladson Monteiro
Sayanee Mukherjee
Karuna Narayanan

**Project Coordinators**
Sanghamitra Deb
Amey Sawant

**Proofreader**
Simran Bhogal

**Indexer**
Rekha Nair

**Graphics**
Disha Haria

**Production Coordinator**
Melwyn D'sa

**Cover Work**
Melwyn D'sa

# Notice

# Citrix® XenApp® 7.x Performance Essentials

Tune and optimize the performance of your farms with the new improved XenApp® architecture

**Luca Dentella**

BIRMINGHAM - MUMBAI

# Citrix® XenApp® 7.x Performance Essentials

First published: August 2013

Second edition: August 2014

Production reference: 1110814

Published by Packt Publishing Ltd.
Livery Place
35 Livery Street
Birmingham B3 2PB, UK.

ISBN 978-1-78217-611-4

www.packtpub.com

Cover image by Pratyush Mohanta (tysoncinematics@gmail.com)

# About the Author

**Luca Dentella** is an IT architect working for an Italian consulting company, Sorint.LAB.

He graduated in Telecommunication Engineering from the Polytechnic University of Milan, and he specialized in Windows and Virtualization technologies, becoming both a Microsoft and a VMware Certified Professional.

Over the last 7 years, he has worked mainly for ING Direct, Italy, where he helped to design, develop, and evolve the IT infrastructure of the bank. Some projects he was involved in include call center virtualization, design of bankshop infrastructures, outsourcing part of the back office, and insourcing the core banking backend.

In the past, he worked as a Java/C# developer. Now, he leverages his programming skills to write scripts and programs to automate administrative tasks.

He designs, implements, and administers XenApp farms for different customers.

He's the author of *Citrix XenApp Performance Essentials*, *Packt Publishing*.

You can visit Luca's blog at `http://www.lucadentella.it`.

Special thanks to my family and my girlfriend, Sara, for supporting me during the writing of this book. Also, I'd like to thank my colleagues for helping me understand the network and security concepts, and my company for providing the lab environment.

# About the Reviewers

**Mark Fermin** is a director and IT solutions architect living in Atlanta, Georgia. His 18-year IT career has allowed him to gain experience in engineering, consulting, architecture, and technical leadership and management. Most recently, his work has focused on solutions architecture in End User Compute, Datacenter Virtualization, Mobility and Consumerization, Application Delivery, Operational Intelligence, and Security and Privacy. While his career experience has spanned many industry verticals, he has specific affinity and passion for designing solutions for healthcare.

Mark's expertise comes from employment with industry leaders and clients, including Microsoft, Citrix Systems®, The Fred Hutchinson Cancer Research Center, Providence Health System, Xerox, Bayer AG, and McKesson Corporation.

Mark was a reviewer for *Getting Started with Citrix VDI-in-a-Box*, *Stuart Arthur Brown*, *Packt Publishing*.

Mark has been an active blogger and contributor to the enterprise IT community (specifically to the Citrix® and application/desktop virtualization communities) through his posts on his personal technology blog, `http://benchtime.wordpress.com`, contributions made through exclusive membership in the Citrix® Partner Technical Experts advisory group, membership and participation in the Atlanta Citrix® User Group, customer and community advisory groups for VMware, Cisco, ExtraHop, and healthcare IT, as well as mobile advisory workgroups.

**Andy Paul** is an accomplished virtualization architect, instructor, and speaker. He has designed and delivered virtualization projects for Fortune 500 companies, public and private healthcare organizations, and higher-education institutions. He has also served as a lead technical trainer, adjunct professor, and guest speaker for multiple organizations.

Andy is currently a virtualization architect as part of the National Infrastructure Practice at OpenSky Corporation, where he serves as the global end user computing subject matter expert, oversees all the VDI architecture, and manages multiple large-enterprise customers.

Andy has also served as a technical reviewer for other XenApp® publications, and he recently finished writing *Citrix® XenApp® 7.5 Desktop Virtualization Solutions*, *Packt Publishing*.

You can visit Andy's blog at www.paultechnologies.com/blog.

I would like to thank my wife, Mandy, for her support and dedication, which inspires me in all of my professional pursuits and keeps me aiming for the stars.

**Anton van Pelt** is a consultant with over 10 years of Citrix® experience. Anton's focus is primarily on Enterprise Mobility solutions such as Citrix® XenMobile®, ShareFile®, and NetScaler®. Nevertheless, his interests extend much further, giving him broad knowledge of complex IT environments. Anton is active in presenting his technical knowledge throughout the community (Citrix® IRC channel, Citrix® Support Forums, NetScaler® KB, and so on) and at various congresses. He is also the co-author of *Enterprise Mobility Management Smackdown* and *User Environment Management Smackdown, PQR*. You can contact Anton at ape@pqr.nl, follow his Twitter handle @antonvanpelt, or follow his blog at http://www.antonvanpelt.com.

# www.PacktPub.com

## Support files, eBooks, discount offers, and more

You might want to visit www.PacktPub.com for support files and downloads related to your book.

Did you know that Packt offers eBook versions of every book published, with PDF and ePub files available? You can upgrade to the eBook version at www.PacktPub.com and as a print book customer, you are entitled to a discount on the eBook copy. Get in touch with us at service@packtpub.com for more details.

At www.PacktPub.com, you can also read a collection of free technical articles, sign up for a range of free newsletters and receive exclusive discounts and offers on Packt books and eBooks.

http://PacktLib.PacktPub.com

Do you need instant solutions to your IT questions? PacktLib is Packt's online digital book library. Here, you can access, read and search across Packt's entire library of books.

## Why subscribe?

- Fully searchable across every book published by Packt
- Copy and paste, print and bookmark content
- On demand and accessible via web browser

## Free access for Packt account holders

If you have an account with Packt at www.PacktPub.com, you can use this to access PacktLib today and view nine entirely free books. Simply use your login credentials for immediate access.

## Instant updates on new Packt books

Get notified! Find out when new books are published by following @PacktEnterprise on Twitter, or the *Packt Enterprise* Facebook page.

# Table of Contents

# Preface

Citrix® XenApp® is an enterprise solution for virtual application delivery. With XenApp®, IT can mobilize Windows apps and, at the same time, reduce costs by centralizing, consolidating, and managing them in the data center.

Critical tasks that system administrators have to perform are designing, deploying, and maintaining infrastructures that perform well; poor performances may have a dramatic impact on a user's experience and satisfaction.

## What this book covers

*Chapter 1, Designing the New FlexCast® Management Architecture*, helps IT architects understand the new FlexCast® Management Architecture adopted in XenApp® 7.5 and design a good infrastructure.

*Chapter 2, Monitor and Optimize Infrastructure – Director and EdgeSight®*, helps XenApp® administrators monitor and tune the infrastructure for best performance, taking advantage of the new tools included in XenApp® 7.5.

*Chapter 3, Monitor and Optimize End User Experience*, helps XenApp® administrators improve the end user experience.

*Chapter 4, Publishing Applications through WAN Links*, helps XenApp® administrators optimize application delivery for mobile and remote users and explains the use of WAN simulators to test the end user experience.

# What you need for this book

This book covers the latest version of Citrix® XenApp® 7.5. While this book was being written, particular attention was given to pointing out the differences from the previous versions and underlining the features available only with a particular licensing.

# Who this book is for

If you are an IT architect or administrator who needs a practical guide that will help you design and optimize the XenApp® infrastructure, this is the book for you.

You will learn how to design, deliver, and maintain a scalable, high-performing XenApp® infrastructure, and the book includes guidelines, tips, and real-world examples to monitor and optimize system loads and user experience.

A chapter is dedicated to mobile and remote users connected through WAN links. Specific configurations and suggestions are included to optimize and test the infrastructure in this scenario. The chapter also covers the use of Citrix® CloudBridge™ as a WAN accelerator.

# Conventions

In this book, you will find a number of styles of text that distinguish between different kinds of information. Here are some examples of these styles, and an explanation of their meaning.

Code words in text, database table names, folder names, filenames, file extensions, pathnames, dummy URLs, user input, and Twitter handles are shown as follows: "Using the Get-BrokerMachine cmdlet, you can obtain objects that represent the broker machines in your infrastructure."

Any command-line input or output is written as follows:

```
C:\>route add 1.0.0.20 mask 255.255.255.255 1.0.0.201
```

**New terms** and **important words** are shown in bold. Words that you see on the screen, in menus, or dialog boxes for example, appear in the text like this: "Select **Properties** from the drop-down menu and click on **Alerts**."

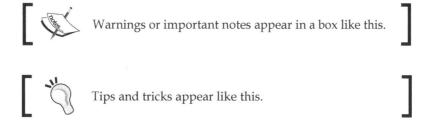

Warnings or important notes appear in a box like this.

Tips and tricks appear like this.

# Reader feedback

Feedback from our readers is always welcome. Let us know what you think about this book—what you liked or may have disliked. Reader feedback is important for us to develop titles that you really get the most out of.

To send us general feedback, simply send an e-mail to feedback@packtpub.com, and mention the book title through the subject of your message.

If there is a topic that you have expertise in and you are interested in either writing or contributing to a book, see our author guide on www.packtpub.com/authors.

# Customer support

Now that you are the proud owner of a Packt book, we have a number of things to help you to get the most from your purchase.

# Errata

Although we have taken every care to ensure the accuracy of our content, mistakes do happen. If you find a mistake in one of our books—maybe a mistake in the text or the code—we would be grateful if you would report this to us. By doing so, you can save other readers from frustration and help us improve subsequent versions of this book. If you find any errata, please report them by visiting http://www.packtpub. com/support, selecting your book, clicking on the **errata submission form** link, and entering the details of your errata. Once your errata are verified, your submission will be accepted and the errata will be uploaded to our website, or added to any list of existing errata, under the Errata section of that title. Any existing errata can be viewed by selecting your title from http://www.packtpub.com/support.

# Piracy

Piracy of copyright material on the Internet is an ongoing problem across all media. At Packt, we take the protection of our copyright and licenses very seriously. If you come across any illegal copies of our works, in any form, on the Internet, please provide us with the location address or website name immediately so that we can pursue a remedy.

Please contact us at copyright@packtpub.com with a link to the suspected pirated material.

We appreciate your help in protecting our authors, and our ability to bring you valuable content.

# Questions

You can contact us at questions@packtpub.com if you are having a problem with any aspect of the book, and we will do our best to address it.

# 1

# Designing the New FlexCast® Management Architecture

The design of a XenApp infrastructure is a complex task that requires good knowledge of XenApp components. Making the right decisions in the design phase may also greatly help system administrators to expand XenApp farms to satisfy new business requirements or to improve the user experience.

In this chapter, you will learn about the following:

- The key features of the new FlexCast Management Architecture
- The five-layer model
- Sizing each layer's components
- Implementing and using Machine Creation Services to deploy new worker servers in minutes
- The difference between XenApp 6.5 and 7.5

## FlexCast® Management Architecture

With XenApp 7.5, Citrix adopted the same architecture that was introduced in XenDesktop 5 and refined in XenDesktop 7, namely, **FlexCast Management Architecture (FMA)**.

FMA is primarily made up of Delivery Controllers and agents. Delivery agents are installed on all virtual and/or physical machines that host and publish resources (named **worker servers**), while the controllers manage users, resources, configurations, and store them in a central SQL server database.

Unlike the previous versions of XenApp, the delivery agent now communicates only with the controllers in the Site and does not need to access the Site's database or license server directly, as illustrated in the following figure:

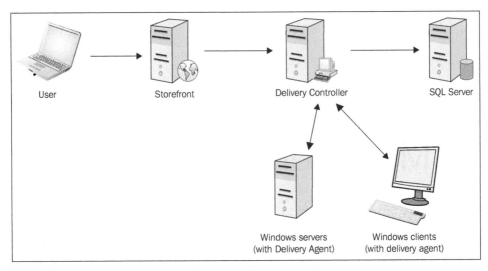

Overview of FlexCast infrastructure's elements

The main advantage of this architectural change is that now only one underlying infrastructure is used by XenApp and XenDesktop. Therefore, the overall solution might include both published applications and virtual desktops, leveraging the same infrastructure elements.

XenApp administrators who have moved to version 7.5 might be a bit confused; there are no more zones or data collectors. By the end of this chapter, you will find a table that maps concepts and terms from XenApp 6.x to the new ones in XenApp 7.5.

# The five-layer model

When designing a new infrastructure, a common mistake is trying to focus on everything at once. A better and suggested approach is to divide the solution into *layers* and then analyze, size, and make decisions, one level at a time.

FlexCast Management Architecture can be divided into the following five layers:

- **User layer**: This defines user groups and locations
- **Access layer**: This defines how users access the resources
- **Resource layer**: This defines which resources are assigned to the given users

- **Control layer**: This defines the components required to run the solution
- **Hardware layer**: This defines the physical elements where the software components run

The power of a FlexCast architecture is that it's extremely flexible; different users can have their own set of policies and resources, but everything is managed by a single, integrated control layer, as shown in the following figure:

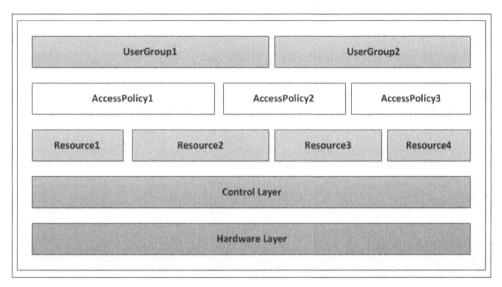

The five-layer model of FlexCast Management Architecture

# The user layer

The need for a new application delivery solution normally comes from user requirements.

The minimum information that must be collected is as follows:

- What users need access to (business applications, a personalized desktop environment, and so on)
- What endpoints the users will use (personal devices, thin clients, smartphones, and so on)
- Where users connect from (company's internal network, unreliable external networks, and so on)

User groups can access more than one resource at a time. For example, office workers can access a shared desktop environment with some common office applications that are installed, and in addition, use some hosted applications.

# The access layer

The access layer defines how users gain access to their resources based on where the user is located and the security policies of the organization.

The infrastructure components that provide access to resources are as follows:

- StoreFront (Web Interface 5.4 is still supported to offer customers additional time to migrate to StoreFront)
- NetScaler Gateway

The following figure demonstrates the access layer:

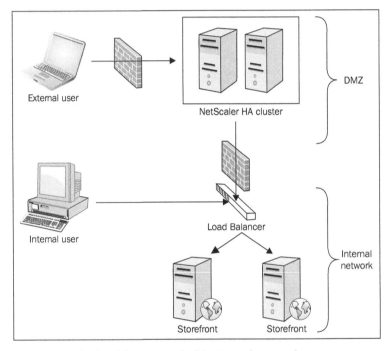

FlexCast Management Architecture — the access layer

# StoreFront

Internal users access a StoreFront store using Citrix Receiver that is installed on their endpoints or via the StoreFront web interface. StoreFront also offers a receiver for HTML5 that does not require any installation on the user's device.

Upon successful authentication, StoreFront contacts a Delivery Controller to receive the list of available resources and allows the users to mark some of them as favorites.

StoreFront requires Windows 2008 R2 SP1 or later, with **Microsoft Internet Information Services (IIS)** and the .NET framework. Even if it can be installed on a server that runs other components, my suggestion is to install it on at least two dedicated servers with a load balancer in front of them to provide high availability.

 Users' subscriptions are automatically synchronized between all the StoreFront servers.

StoreFront is the entry point of your XenApp infrastructure. To correctly size its servers, you will need to estimate or measure the maximum number of concurrent logins (if your infrastructure mainly serves internal users, most of the logins will happen in the morning, when users arrive at office).

From my experience, StoreFront does not require a lot of hardware resources: a server with two CPUs and 4 GB of memory is enough for up to 1,000 user connections per hour.

# NetScaler Gateway™

Remote users connect and authenticate to NetScaler Gateway, which is located within the network's DMZ.

 NetScaler Gateway is available both as a hardware appliance (MPX) and a virtual appliance (VPX); the virtual appliance delivers the same features and functionalities as that of the physical one. The main difference between VPX and MPX is about SSL; MPX has dedicated offload capabilities.
An MPX appliance has a single, dual-core processor and 4 GB of memory, while the virtual appliance that can be run on VMware ESXi, Microsoft Hyper-V, and XenServer, requires at least 2 virtual CPUs, 4 GB of memory and 20 GB of disk space.

NetScaler Gateway establishes a secure SSL channel with the user's device, and all the traffic is encapsulated in that channel.

Upon successful validation, NetScaler forwards the user request to the internal StoreFront servers that then generates a list of the available resources that is passed back to the user through NetScaler Gateway.

When the user launches a resource, all the traffic between the server that hosts the resource and the user's device is again encapsulated in the SSL channel.

To provide high availability, you can deploy two NetScaler Gateway appliances in a *failover* clustering configuration; so, if the primary active appliance fails, the secondary one becomes active. The HA feature is native and part of the NetScaler license; it does not require any external clustering solutions (Microsoft Cluster…).

## Access policies

In most environments, there are different security policies based on the users' locations; for example, users in the internal network can authenticate using only the username and password, while external users might need to enter a token code as well (multifactor authentication).

In NetScaler Gateway, you can configure session policies to differentiate between incoming connections by analyzing elements such as IP addresses, HTTP headers, SSL certificates, and so on. Moreover, you can also combine different expressions using logical operators (OR and AND), use built-in functions to test whether the client is running the most updated antivirus, and perform string matching with the power of regular expressions.

Policies do not take actions. They provide the *logic* to evaluate traffic. To perform an operation based on a policy's evaluation, you have to configure **actions** and **profiles** and associate them with policies. Policies can be applied at user, group, and server levels; all the applicable policies are inspected, and the one with the lowest priority wins.

Actions are steps that NetScaler takes; for example, you can allow an incoming connection if it matches the associated policy and deny it if not.

Profiles are collections of settings, for example, the session timeout (in minutes) or the Web interface / Storefront server URL.

To help system administrators create the correct policies and profiles for most common clients (Citrix Receiver, Receiver for Web, Clientless Access, and so on), **Quick Configuration Wizard** is automatically executed the first time you configure NetScaler Gateway.

# The resource layer

A XenApp infrastructure is designed and implemented to offer resources to the users.

XenApp offers different strategies to deliver applications. The choice of the correct strategy has a high impact on the infrastructure. Later in this chapter, you'll learn how to size the servers based on the number and type of applications.

# Hosted apps

Hosting apps is the most common strategy: applications are installed and published on servers with a delivery agent installed (worker servers). Each application is assigned to a delivery group; when accessed, the application executes on the hosting server, and the user interface is displayed on the user's desktop. This is the best approach for standard, business applications.

# VM-hosted apps

Some applications might not run on server-based operating systems such as Windows 2012. They have particular license or software requirements that conflict with other installed applications. Using the VM-hosted apps strategy, these applications are installed on virtual machines based on client-operating systems (such as Windows 7). When a user requires one of the applications, it runs on the VM, and its user interface is displayed on the user's desktop.

Because applications are installed on a client-operating system that does not support more than one user connected at a time, you need at least one VM for each concurrent execution of the hosted application.

# Streamed apps

Applications are not installed on the server or user's desktop. Using a solution such as Microsoft App-V or VMware ThinApp, they are dynamically delivered to the target server or desktop when accessed. Such solutions require an external infrastructure. They are normally chosen when there are a large number of different applications to be delivered or when applications are resource-intensive; therefore, they must be run on the end user's device. Applications have to be carefully evaluated and packaged prior to streaming; refer to Microsoft and VMware's documentation for more detailed information.

# Shared desktops

Users connect to a hosted server-based Windows operating system where the virtual machine is shared among a pool of users simultaneously. In this scenario, each user is encapsulated within their own session, and the desktop interface is remotely displayed.

# Remote PC Access

Users connect to their physical office desktops, allowing them to work at any time. **Remote PC Access** uses the Citrix HDX policies and access layer, providing better security and performance over a simple RDP connection. Moreover, the connections can be managed using the centralized delivery console.

# The control layer

The control layer includes all the components that are required to run the infrastructure:

- Delivery Controllers
- SQL databases
- License servers

# Delivery Controllers

A **Delivery Controller** is responsible for distributing applications and desktops, managing user access, and optimizing connections to applications. Each Site has one or more Delivery Controllers.

A Delivery Controller is the heart of a XenApp infrastructure; it is queried when a user logs in, when it launches an application, and when policies are evaluated. It's therefore important to correctly size the servers that host this component.

The minimum requirements are as follows:

- 2 vCPU and 4 GB of memory
- 100 MB of disk space to install the software
- Windows 2008 R2 Service Pack 1 or later

In my experience, Delivery Controllers consume a lot of CPU memory; this is especially true in those moments of the day (for example, in the morning) when most of the users start working. If the CPU of the Delivery Controllers' servers reaches a critical threshold, roughly 80 percent, you need to scale up or scale out.

If you're using a virtualized environment, it could be easy to add virtual CPUs to the servers; an alternative is to add another controller to the Site configuration.

Your infrastructure should have at least two Delivery Controllers to provide high availability. You can add more Delivery Controllers and the load will be evenly distributed across all the controllers, thus helping to reduce the overall load on each single controller.

In a virtualized environment, the controllers should be distributed across multiple physical servers to help spread the CPU load across multiple servers and provide greater levels of fault tolerance. On VMware, for example, you can configure an **anti-affinity rule** to ensure the virtual servers would never be placed on the same physical one.

# SQL databases

All the configuration settings, the log of changes, and the monitoring events of your XenApp infrastructure are stored in SQL databases.

XenApp 7.5 supports the following Microsoft SQL Server versions:

- SQL Server 2008 R2 SP2 Express, Standard, Enterprise, and Datacenter editions
- SQL Server 2012 SP1 Express, Standard, Enterprise, and Datacenter editions

If no SQL Server is found, SQL Server 2012 SP1 Express Edition is installed during the installation of the first controller of your Site. The use of the free Express Edition is, however, suitable only for small installations (less than 100 users).

 To provide high availability, XenApp 7.5 supports the following SQL Server features:

- Clustered instances
- Mirroring
- AlwaysOn Availability Groups (SQL Server 2012 only)

By default, the **Configuration Logging** and **Monitoring** databases (usually called as the secondary databases) are located on the same server as the **Site Configuration** database. Initially, a single database is used for all the three datastores, as shown in the following screenshot:

## Databases

| Datastore | Database Name | Server Address | Mirror Server Addr... |
|---|---|---|---|
| Site | CitrixLabSite | XA-CTRL01\SQLEXPRESS | |
| Logging | CitrixLabSite | XA-CTRL01\SQLEXPRESS | |
| Monitoring | CitrixLabSite | XA-CTRL01\SQLEXPRESS | |

The Site, Logging, and Monitoring databases

# The Site database

The **Site** database contains configuration information on how the system runs.

Its size and load increases during peak hours as each user logon requires multiple transactions to be carried out. It also generates session and connection information to be tracked.

If the Site database becomes unavailable, the system is unable to accept new users, while the existing connections are maintained.

Delivery Controllers don't have **Local Host Cache** (**LHC**) like the datastore servers had in previous versions of XenApp. Thanks to LHC, the infrastructure could be run even if the database server is unavailable; with the absence of LHC in XenApp 7.5, the database server has become a more critical element of the infrastructure.

The maximum size is usually reached after 48 hours as a small log of connections is maintained within the Site database for two days.

From my experience, the Site database does not require much storage. A typical storage requirement is as follows (refer to `http://support.citrix.com/article/CTX139508`):

| Number of users | Number of applications | Database size |
| --- | --- | --- |
| 100 | 50 | 50 MB |
| 100 | 250 | 150 MB |
| 1,000 | 50 | 70 MB |

# Monitoring database

The **Monitoring** database contains historical information used by the Director.

The retention period depends on the XenApp license you own:

- For *non-platinum* customers, the default and maximum period is seven days
- For *platinum* customers, the default period is 90 days with no maximum period

Updates to the Monitoring database are performed in batches and the number of transactions per second is usually low (less than 20). Overnight processing is performed to remove obsolete data.

If the Monitoring database becomes unavailable, the system works but data is not collected and not visible within Director.

Of the three databases, the Monitoring database is expected to grow the largest over time. Its size depends on many factors; anyway, a realistic estimation is that 1,000 users working 5 days/week generate 20-30 MB of data each week.

## The Configuration Logging database

The **Configuration Logging** database contains a historical log of all the configuration changes. The information is used by audit reports.

The size and transaction rate are hard to predict; they depend on how much configuration activity is performed. This is usually the smallest and least-loaded database of the three.

The Configuration Logging database has no retention policy; here, data is not removed unless done so manually by the administrator.

The administrator can configure the Site database to accept or refuse configuration changes when the Configuration Logging database is unavailable, as shown in the following screenshot:

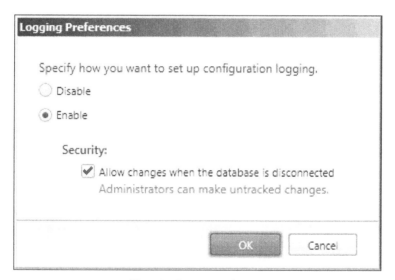

Changing logging preferences

## Moving databases

Citrix recommends that you change the location of the secondary databases after you create a Site database.

You can simply change the location of the databases from Studio, as follows:

1. Select **Configuration** on the left-hand side of the pane.
2. Select the database you want to change the location for.
3. Click on **Change Database** in the **Actions** pane.
4. Specify the location of the new database server.

If you specify a new location, remember that the data in the previous database is not imported to the new one and that logs cannot be aggregated from both the databases.

You can also *migrate* the databases from the actual database server to the new one without losing data. First, you must stop configuration logging and monitoring to make sure that no new data is written to the database during the move.

Then, start Windows PowerShell and type the following commands:

```
PS C:\> asnp Citrix*
PS C:\> Set-LogSite -State "Disabled"
PS C:\> Set-MonitorConfiguration -DataCollectionEnabled $False
```

Now, you can back up the existing databases and restore them onto the new server.

After having configured the new database location as explained earlier, remember to enable configuration logging and monitoring again with the following commands:

```
PS C:\> Set-LogSite -State "Enabled"
PS C:\> Set-MonitorConfiguration -DataCollectionEnabled $True
```

The asnp part means Add-PSSnapin; this means that the first line loads the Citrix-specific PowerShell modules, and it's required to run PowerShell commands and scripts that interact with Citrix products.

## Scaling

If your infrastructure grows and more controllers are brought online, the SQL database CPU will eventually become a bottleneck.

To expand the size of a single XenApp installation, you can opt for one of the following options:

- **Divide**: This is used to move secondary databases to a new server.
- **Scale up**: This is used to add additional CPU resources to your database server.

- **Scale out**: This is used to create a second XenApp Site alongside the initial one. Note that each Site would be semi-independent of each other; some components may be shared (such as the access layer), but the controllers and the SQL databases would only function within their own Site.

# License servers

The license server stores and manages Citrix licenses. The first time a user connects to a XenApp server, the server checks out a license for the user, and subsequent connections of the same user share the same license.

A single license server is enough for Sites with thousands of servers and users; you could install a second license server in your Site, but the two servers cannot share licenses. Because the license server is contacted when the user connects to a XenApp server, slow responses will ensue and might increase the login time. You should place the license service on a dedicated server or, in the case of smaller infrastructures, on a server that doesn't publish applications. The license server process is single-threaded, so multiple processors do not increase its performance.

If the license server is not available, all the servers in your Site enter a grace period of 720 hours; during this period, users are still allowed to connect. This means that you usually don't need a high-availability solution for your license server; if a server fault occurs, you can install a new license server during the 30 days of the grace period or power on a second license server you prepared and kept turned off (cold standby).

# The hardware layer

The hardware layer is the physical implementation of the XenApp solution. After having collected all of the required information for previous layers, we're now ready to choose the correct number of servers and their hardware configuration.

The two different sets of hardware are defined as follows:

- One for the resource layer
- One for the access and control layers

# Hosting resources

For server-hosted resources (hosted apps, shared desktops, and VM-hosted apps), a set of physical or virtual machines is required.

VM-hosted apps run on client-operating systems, and each user must be provided with a dedicated machine; therefore, the number of machines depend on the number of concurrent users. For hosted apps or shared desktops, the number of servers you need and their hardware configuration depends on the number of users and applications, and even more on the kind of the applications and how you deliver them to the users.

The use of a virtual infrastructure is highly recommended; it lets you quickly reallocate resources (CPU, memory, and so on) if required. Later in this chapter, you'll learn how to use a new delivery fabric solution by Citrix, **Machine Creation Services** (**MCS**), to deploy new servers in minutes, working together with your virtualization technology.

My suggestion for correctly sizing your infrastructure is to set up a test environment where you can verify the load that each application produces using real users or automatic testing tools such as LoginVSI or HP Loadrunner (Citrix EdgeSight for load testing is now deprecated and no longer supported).

> With XenApp 7.5, the hardware layer can also include cloud-hosted desktops and apps with the integration of Amazon AWS, CloudPlatform, and Microsoft Azure.
>
> Amazon AWS only supports Server OS machines.

I found out that the new delivery agent is lighter in weight than the IMA service installed on session host servers in XenApp 6.5; therefore, you might save some hardware resources when moving to the new 7.5 version.

# Applications on servers – siloed versus nonsiloed

Two strategies for placing hosted applications on servers are available: **siloed** and **nonsiloed**.

## Siloed

In this approach, applications are installed on small groups of servers; you could even have the servers running a single application. Applications are usually grouped by their use; for example, all the applications used by the Finance department are installed on the same servers, while the applications used by the HR department are installed on different servers.

This approach is sometimes required if your applications have different hardware requirements or might cause conflicts if installed on the same server. Some application vendors, moreover, don't consider a different licensing agreement if their applications are published through XenApp. So, if you pay licensing fees, by simply counting the number of installations, you might reduce the cost of installing them on a small number of servers.

Siloed applications can increase costs as they require more resources for standby; they require more hot spare servers (at least one for each silo) than the nonsiloed approach. If silos are necessary for isolation, you can consider using app streaming.

## Nonsiloed

In this approach, all the applications are installed on all the servers. This approach is more efficient as it reduces the number of required servers, and it may also improve the user experience because it allows users to share the same server session with different applications. If you're using any automatic technology to deploy servers, a nonsiloed approach will also help you to reduce the number of different images you have to create and maintain.

My suggestion is to use the nonsiloed approach when possible. Later in this book, you'll learn that with session machine catalogs and delivery groups, you will still be able to logically group applications on servers even with this approach.

# Supporting the infrastructure

A typical XenApp 7.5 infrastructure has a couple of Storefront servers, a couple of Delivery Controllers, one license server, and one database server (clustered to provide high availability). If you have external users, a VPN solution (NetScaler Gateway or third-party products) is usually added.

When sizing the infrastructure, consider that Storefront and Delivery Controller servers can be easily scaled out by adding new servers, while you can't have two active database servers in your Site to balance the load or add another database server to your Site. Moreover, if you're using a shared database server (for example, a database server that is also hosting some production databases), pay attention to the fact that the load generated by XenApp will not be smooth during the day, but it will probably have peaks in the morning and after lunchtime.

Even if Citrix supports the installation of a Delivery Controller, license server, and Storefront on the same server (and this is the default option during the setup), my suggestion is, wherever possible, to use different servers; better if these servers are virtualized. If your virtualized environment has built-in HA functionalities (such as VMware HA or Hyper-V clustering), you might deploy only one Delivery Controller and one Storefront server to start and then add new servers if needed.

# Storage

Storage is often considered as one of the most important and complex decisions in a XenApp or XenDesktop solution.

Storage is not only the amount of disk space that must be allocated to the solution but also the number of **Input/Output Operations (IOPS)** that must be available in order to provide a good user experience.

It might seem strange at first, but when you're choosing the correct storage solution for your new infrastructure, the most critical information is the maximum number of IOPS the storage platform you're evaluating can offer. All the storage systems can indeed be updated to add more disk space, while the maximum number of IOPS can be limited by the type of connection (fiber-channel, iSCSI, and so on), its speed, or the storage controllers, elements that are difficult or expensive to replace when in production.

As a rule of thumb, you can consider 10-15 IOPS for each virtual desktop-running office applications and 5-8 IOPS for each user-running applications on worker servers.

 You can use the free **Iometer** tool (http://www.iometer.org) to test the performance of your storage's subsystem.

An example of using the Iometer tool is shown in the following screenshot:

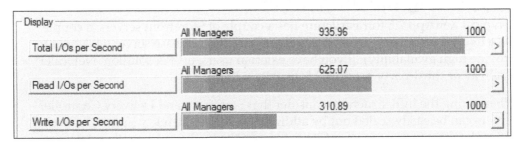

Using Iometer to test the maximum number of IOPS

# Machine Creation Services

Infrastructures are not static; they evolve to satisfy new business requirements, offer new applications, or support new users.

A common task that every Citrix administrator has to face is to deploy, as fast as he or she can, new worker servers. Citrix offers the following two technologies to automatically provide new servers, starting with a *master* image:

- Provisioning Services (PVS)
- Machine Creation Services (MCS)

**Provisioning Services** is a classic solution, available for years and widely used in many XenApp and XenDesktop infrastructures.

Servers are delivered from a Provisioning Services virtual disk (vDisk), imaged from a master device. Target servers are configured to perform a network boot and receive the vDisk image from the PVS server. vDisks are usually configured in the read-only mode; local changes are discarded at every reboot.

Provisioning Services works with almost any device and does not require any virtualization technology. The target servers can be physical, virtual, or a mix of both.

Machine Creation Services was introduced in XenDesktop 5, and now, with the adoption of FlexCast Management Architecture, it is also available for XenApp infrastructures.

It leverages on a virtualization technology to deploy and control the full life cycle of virtual servers and virtual desktops, starting with a master virtual machine.

# PVS versus MCS

Both Provisioning Services and Machine Creation Services are enterprise solutions included in XenApp 7.5.

PVS is the only choice if you're going to implement physical targets. MCS integrates on the hypervisor layer and therefore cannot be used on physical servers.

PVS is usually preferable in a mixed infrastructure that also includes a large number (less than 2,000) of virtual desktops. PVS is also preferable because MCS requires more IOPS (about 21 percent) than PVS and potentially more storage space.

Persistency, that is, the need to maintain changes for different targets forced the use of MCS in the past. The reason was that PVS prior to version 6.0 only had *server-side* caching that caused several performance issues. Now, both the technologies offer *client-side* caching.

For small and midsize XenApp infrastructures, with only virtual servers, my choice is MCS now; this is because of the following reasons:

- It does not require any dedicated servers like PVS does
- It takes advantage of virtualization features such as snapshots
- It is integrated in Citrix Studio (PVS requires a dedicated console)
- It does not use the network to deploy the servers (PVS can generate high traffic on the network)

# IOPS and IntelliCache

Citrix documented that MCS generates approximately 45 percent of more peak IOPS compared to PVS. The reason is that during the boot and logon phases, all the virtual machines created by MCS access a shared copy of the master image, and servers that are provisioned by PVS get the needed data through the network instead.

The typical R/W (read/write) ratio for Windows MCS machines during the various phases is as shown in the following diagram:

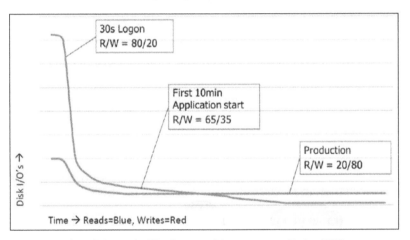

The R/W ratio for Windows machines, courtesy: Project VRC

If you're using XenServer (from Version 5.6 Feature Pack 1), you take advantage of the **IntelliCache** feature to reduce the number of IOPS performed on your storage.

After the first start of a virtual machine, IntelliCache uses the local storage cache of the server to cache blocks of the base image as far as they are accessed by the virtual desktop. If a second VM is started on the host, it uses the already cached bits on local storage and does not need to reach out to the shared storage.

IntelliCache also caches temporary and nonpersistent files; this means that a portion of a runtime read/write of each virtual machine might occur in a low cost server-attached storage rather than the consumption of IOPS resources of your storage area's network.

First, you have to enable IntelliCache when installing XenServer, choosing **Enable thin provisioning (Optimized storage for XenDesktop)**.

> You can also enable thin provisioning on an existing XenServer; refer to Citrix's installation guide (`http://support.citrix.com/article/CTX129387`).

IntelliCache is disabled by default in XenApp or XenDesktop. When you are adding a XenServer host and are prompted for the type of storage to use, select **Shared**; then, select **Use IntelliCache to reduce load on the shared storage device**, as shown in the following screenshot:

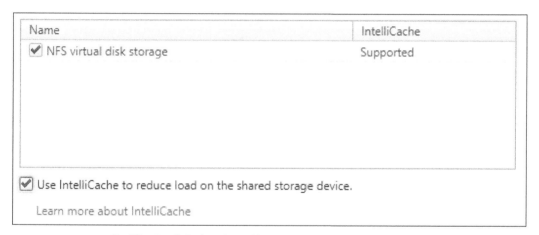

| Name | IntelliCache |
| --- | --- |
| ✔ NFS virtual disk storage | Supported |

✔ Use IntelliCache to reduce load on the shared storage device.

Learn more about IntelliCache

Enabling IntelliCache when adding a XenServer host to Citrix Studio

> VMware vSphere 5 includes a feature named **Content-Based Read Cache (CBRC)** that is similar to IntelliCache. With this feature, you can have the host hypervisor scan the storage disk blocks to generate digests of the block contents. When these blocks are read into the hypervisor, they are cached in the host-based CBRC, and subsequent reads of blocks with the same digest are served from the in-memory cache directly.
>
> Even if CBRC is not officially supported by Citrix, it can be used to optimize IO workloads when using MCS with VMware virtual infrastructures.

# Requirements

Machine Creation Services require one of the following virtualization technologies:

- Citrix XenServer 6.0.2 or higher
- VMware vSphere 5.0 update 2 or higher
- System Center Virtual Machine Manager 2012 or higher (includes any version of Hyper-V that can register with the supported System Center Virtual Machine Manager versions)

Machine Creation Services can also deploy virtual machines on **Amazon Web Services** (**AWS**) and Citrix CloudPlatform.

The following virtualization technology and storage-type combinations are supported; combinations in bold are recommended:

| Virtualization technology | Local disks | NFS | Block storage |
|---|---|---|---|
| XenServer | Yes | **Yes** | Yes |
| VMware | Yes | **Yes** | Yes |
| Hyper-V | Yes | No | **Yes** (with cluster-shared volumes) |

# Connecting to the virtual infrastructure

MCS requires a connection to your virtual infrastructure.

Open Citrix Studio and select **Hosting** on the left-hand side pane. From the **Actions** pane, click on **Add Connection and Resources**.

Select the hypervisor you're using and enter the credentials for the connection, as shown in the following screenshot:

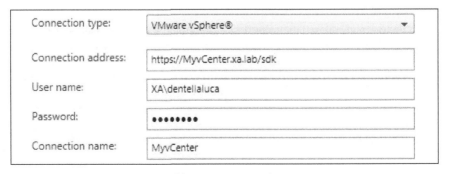

Adding a new connection

Select the resources (cluster, network, and storage) for the new connection and complete the wizard.

 If you're using self-signed SSL certificates in your VMware vCenter, you might encounter an error message: **Cannot connect to the vCenter server due to a certificate error**.

The SSL certificate of the default **Certification Authority (CA)** must be added to Certificate Store of your server, as shown in the following steps:

1. Connect to your vCenter server and copy the `cacert.pem` file from `C:\ProgramData\VMware\VMware VirtualCenter\SSL`.

2. Open Microsoft Management Console (`mmc.exe`) in your controller server and add the **Certificates** snap-in to manage certificates for the local computer account.

3. Import the `cacert.pem` file in the **Trusted Root Certification Authorities** folder, as shown in the following screenshot:

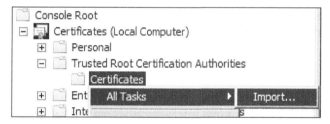

Adding a Trusted Root Certification Authorities certificate

# Creating a new master image

A master image is a template that you can use to deploy your environment. It should contain all the applications and resources you want to deliver using XenApp.

 If you're using Microsoft KMS (Key Management Services) to manage Windows and Office licenses, you don't need to manually launch the rearm process (`slmgr.vbs`) or run the `sysprep.exe` command on the master image.

Create a new virtual machine using the management tool for your hypervisor and install the operating system, including service packs and updates. The number of vCPUs and the amount of memory you assign to the virtual machine is not critical; you can change these settings when you create a machine catalog. It's important to choose the correct amount of disk space, including the space that will be required for applications and users' data (if you're not using a profile management solution) because it cannot be changed later.

Install the integration tools for your hypervisor (VMware Tools, XenServer Tools, and Hyper-V Integration Services); then, install the Citrix **Virtual Delivery Agent (VDA)**.

When installing VDA, select **Create a Master Image**, enter the addresses of your Delivery Controllers, and enable the **Optimize performance** feature, as shown in the following screenshot:

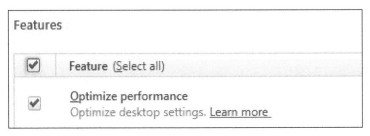

Enabling the Optimize performance feature

Install and configure the applications you're going to deliver using XenApp and any third-party tools needed in your infrastructure, such as antivirus software or management agents. Make sure those tools can be installed in machines deployed from a single image; some agents create a **unique identifier (UUID)** when you install them, and if all your servers are created from a single installation, they'll have the same UUID. Sometimes, you might need to write a startup script for your servers that will change the agent's UUID (usually stored in Windows Registry).

When the master image is complete, Citrix recommends that you create a snapshot of it and name the snapshot so that you can identify the master image in future. If you specify a master image rather than a snapshot when creating a machine catalog, Studio creates a snapshot for you but you cannot name it.

# Creating a machine catalog

Machine catalogs are collections of physical or virtual machines that you can assign to users.

A machine catalog can be configured to use MCS to create the number of VMs you specify based on the master image you created in previous sections.

In Citrix Studio, select **Machine Catalogs** on the left-hand side pane and then click on **Create Machine Catalog** in the **Actions** pane.

Select the appropriate operating system for your machine catalog; if you're going to deliver applications using XenApp, choose **Windows Server OS**.

You're now prompted to select the machine management tool that your catalog will use. Choose **Machines that are power managed** (this means you want to use a machine management tool) and **Deploy machines using Citrix Machine Creation Service**, as shown in the following screenshot:

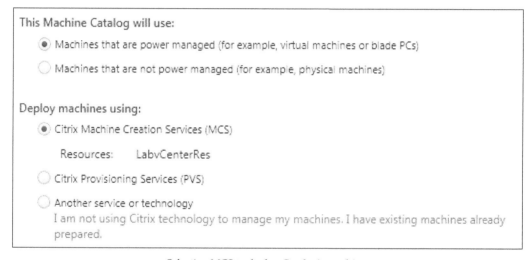

Selecting MCS to deploy Catalog's machines

Select the virtual machine (or one of its snapshots) that will become the master image of your catalog:

Define the number of virtual machines needed in the new catalog along with their resources, as shown in the following screenshot (the number of vCPUs and the amount of memory). Note that the hard disk size cannot be changed.

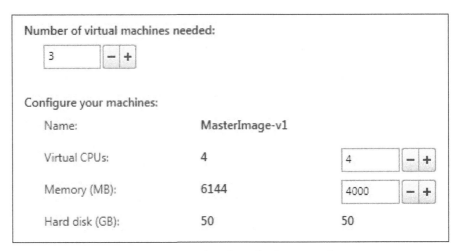

Defining the virtual machines for the new catalog

The new virtual machines require an Active Directory computer account. If you have access to an Active Directory domain admin account, you can allow Studio to create new accounts for you by performing the following steps:

1. Select the location where the computer accounts will be created. I suggest that you should create a dedicated **Organizational Unit (OU)** in your domain; a dedicated OU also allows you to apply specific policies to the servers from within.

2. Specify the account-naming scheme.

If you can't create accounts in your Active Directory, you can select unused accounts that already exist (or that someone created for you), or you can import a .csv file that contains the list of account names in the following form:

```
[ADComputerAccount]
accountname1.domain
accountname2.domain
```

MCS can reset the account passwords, or if all the accounts share the same password, you can specify it.

**Account-naming scheme**

This scheme can consist of fixed characters and a variable part defined by the # characters. A scheme can include only one variable part, and you can define it to be either numeric (1, 2,…) or alphabetic (A, B,…). The number of hash characters defines the minimum length of the variable region; for example, a naming scheme of `WorkServer##` will result in accounts called WorkServers01, WorkServer02 or WorkServerAA, WorkServerAB.

The characters not allowed in a naming scheme are \, / ,:, *, ?, ", <, >, |, , , ~, !, @, $, %, ^, &, ', (, ), {, }, and _.

If your master image has more than one network card, you can enable/disable the network cards and associate them to the correct virtual network.

At the end of the wizard, MCS copies the master image to the datastores you configured as resources for the connection to your virtual infrastructure and creates the requested number of virtual machines.

Machine Catalog is now ready to deliver applications, as shown in the following screenshot:

| Search results for '(Machine Catalog Is "MCSCatalog")' | | |
|---|---|---|
| Desktop OS Machines (0) | **Server OS Machines (3)** | Sessions (0) |
| Name | Machine Catalog | Delivery Group |
| XA-WORKER01.xa.lab | MCSCatalog | - |
| XA-WORKER02.xa.lab | MCSCatalog | - |
| XA-WORKER03.xa.lab | MCSCatalog | - |

Machine Catalog managed by MCS

You can use the **Test Machine Catalog** action to verify that the new Machine Catalog is properly configured.

# Updating machines

If you need to perform an update (for example, install OS patches) or install new applications, you can perform the requested changes on the master image, take a new snapshot (so you can always return to the previous image if something goes wrong), and with a configurable rollout strategy, update the catalog's virtual machines based on the new snapshot.

After having updated the master image, choose the catalog to be updated and select **Update Machines** from the **Actions** pane.

Select the new snapshot and define a rollout strategy, either in the following situations:

- On the next shutdown
- Immediately (shut down and restart the machine now)

If you chose **Immediately**, you can program a distribution time (that is the interval within which the machines are restarted) and send a notification message to the users (for example, warning them to close all the running applications).

# XenApp® 7.5 versus previous versions

Many XenApp administrators who worked with previous versions of XenApp were a bit confused when Citrix decided to adopt the same FlexCast Management Architecture that was introduced in XenDesktop 7 for XenApp 7.5.

In the following table, I have listed the most common functional elements and their corresponding elements (sometimes, they are not exact equivalents) in the newer version:

| XenApp 6.0 | XenApp 7.5 |
| --- | --- |
| Independent Management Architecture (IMA) | FlexCast Management Architecture (FMA) |
| Farm | Delivery Site (or just "Site") |
| Worker group | Session Machine Catalog plus Delivery Group |
| Session-host server | Worker with virtual delivery agent |
| Zone and data collector | Delivery Controller |
| Delivery Services Console | Citrix Studio and Citrix Director |
| Publishing applications | Delivering application |
| Datastore | SQL Server database |
| Load evaluator | Load Management Policy |

# Summary

With XenApp 7.5, Citrix adopted the new FlexCast Management Architecture that was previously introduced for XenDesktop, and now your solution might include both published applications and virtual desktops, leveraging on the same management infrastructure.

A XenApp architecture is made by several components: StoreFront servers, NetScaler Access Gateways, Delivery Controllers, license servers, worker servers, and database servers. All contribute to the correct working of the solution. In this chapter, you learned how to correctly size them based on your business requirements and how to design an infrastructure based on the five-layer model.

If you need to deploy several worker servers, you should consider using Citrix Machine Creation Services. With this tool, you can create a master virtual image of your server and use it to provision as many servers as you need. Day-by-day management is also made easier; updates, patches, and changes have to be applied to the master image only.

If you're an experienced XenApp administrator and have worked with previous versions of XenApp, the new FlexCast Management Architecture may be confusing; at the end of this chapter, I have included a table comparing the terms and technologies of the older versions with the new ones introduced in XenApp 7.5.

In the next chapter, you'll learn how to monitor and optimize the infrastructure when in production.

# 2

# Monitor and Optimize Infrastructure – Director and EdgeSight®

The XenApp infrastructure you designed is now in production. The job of a system administrator starts now; the infrastructure must be monitored and maintained. In addition, problems that were unpredictable in the design phase might appear or new business requirements might arise, increasing the load of your site.

In this chapter, you'll learn about the following topics:

- Performance counters available for the different components of your architecture
- Using Citrix cmdlets for Microsoft PowerShell
- Features offered by the new Citrix Director to monitor and troubleshoot
- Optimizing your worker servers and load balancing the users among them

## Citrix® performance monitoring counters

When you install XenApp on a Windows server, the setup adds some new performance counters that you can access from Windows Performance Monitor. A regular analysis of performance data helps to identify possible bottlenecks or lack of free resources.

It's difficult to define which values are good for the counters in advance; this usually depends on the size of the infrastructure, the number of connected users, and so on. A better approach is to record the values during normal conditions (baselining) and compare the actual values with the baseline.

Citrix performance counters are grouped into six sections. In the next section, you will find descriptions of the most significant counters.

# Citrix® Broker Agent

The following counters are available on desktops and servers where Citrix Delivery Agent is installed:

| Counter name | Description |
|---|---|
| Average Message Payload To Broker Asynchronous/ Synchronous | The average size of asynchronous and synchronous messages sent to Citrix Broker Service (running on Delivery Controllers) |
| Total Message Payload To Broker Asynchronous/Synchronous | The total size of asynchronous and synchronous messages sent to Citrix Broker Service |
| Message Count To Broker Asynchronous/Synchronous | The number of asynchronous and synchronous messages sent to Citrix Broker Service |
| Average Message Payload To Plugins Asynchronous/ Synchronous | The average size of asynchronous and synchronous messages sent to Citrix Plugins (running on client devices) |
| Total Message Payload To Plugins Asynchronous/ Synchronous | The total size of asynchronous and synchronous messages sent to Citrix Plugins |
| Message Count To Plugins Asynchronous/Synchronous | The number of asynchronous and synchronous messages sent to Citrix Plugins |
| Number Of Registration/ Deregistration | The number of registrations and deregistrations that occurred between the Delivery Agent and a Delivery Controller |
| Total App/Desktop Sessions | The number of active XenApp/XenDesktop sessions |
| Total Sessions | The total number of active sessions |

# Citrix® Profile Management

Citrix Profile Management is the Citrix component installed with the Delivery Agent that manages user profiles. The following counters can be useful to analyze slowness in the logon/logoff process:

| Counter name | Description |
|---|---|
| Local Profile Setup Duration | The time (in milliseconds) Windows takes to prepare the local user profile. |
| Logon/Logoff Duration | The total duration (in milliseconds) of the logon and logoff processes. |
| Logon/Logoff Bytes | The amount of data (in bytes) transferred during the logon and logoff processes. |
| Delete Local Profile Duration | If configured, Citrix Profile Management deletes the local profile during logoff. This counter tracks the total duration (in milliseconds) of this process. |
| Processed Logon/Logoff Files | 12 counters (6 for the logon process and 6 for the logoff process) keep track of the number of processed files, depending on the following sizes:<br><br>• Under 1 KB<br><br>• 1 KB to 10 KB<br><br>• 10 KB to 100 KB<br><br>• 100 KB to 1 MB<br><br>• 1 MB to 5 MB<br><br>• Above 5 MB |

# Database counters

In *Chapter 1*, *Designing the New FlexCast® Management Architecture*, you learned that most of the components of your Citrix infrastructure depend on the database server. Each component, therefore, now offers performance counters about its connection to the database server, as shown in the following table:

| Counter name | Description |
|---|---|
| Database Average Transaction Time | The average duration (in seconds) for database transactions |
| Database Connected | Indicates whether the service/component is in contact with the database (value 1) or not (value 0) |
| Database Transactions/sec | The number of successful transactions per second |
| Database Transaction Errors/sec | The number of failing transactions per second |

# Broker Service

The Broker Service, running on Delivery Controllers, manages desktops and worker services. Performance counters are available to measure the number of registrations (when a new device running the Delivery Agent contacts the Broker Service), deregistrations, and brokered sessions.

# XML Service

The XML Service, running on Delivery Controllers, is contacted during the logon process and when users launch applications or desktops.

Three counters are available, which are as follows:

| Counter name | Description |
| --- | --- |
| Average Transaction Time | The average duration (in seconds) for the selected type of XML transaction |
| Concurrent Transactions | The number of concurrent XML transactions |
| Transactions/sec | The number of transactions per second |

In the **Instances** list, you can select the transactions you want to inspect. The preceding counters can be applied to all the XML transactions or to particular transactions, as shown in the following screenshot:

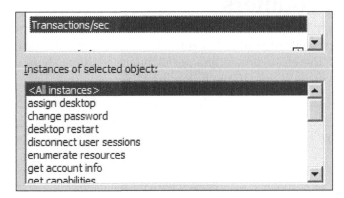

Selecting XML transactions

# Monitoring using Microsoft PowerShell

XenApp provides an SDK based on Microsoft Windows PowerShell Version 3.0.

Using Citrix cmdlets and snap-ins, you can perform the same tasks as you would with the management console (Citrix Studio). Moreover, you can also write PowerShell scripts that retrieve performance or health data from your Citrix infrastructure to integrate with your external monitoring tool.

For example, I used PowerShell scripts to monitor XenApp installations with Nagios, a widely-used open source monitoring tool.

> The PowerShell SDK is compatible only with XenDesktop 5.0 or later. Snap-in names end with V1 or V2; they denote the following versions:
> - V1 is for XenDesktop 5
> - V2 is for XenDesktop 7 or later and for XenApp 7.5

In *Chapter 1*, *Designing the New FlexCast® Management Architecture*, you learned the following command to import all the Citrix plugins:

```
PS C:\> asnp Citrix*
```

This command must be at the top of every script that uses Citrix commands.

In the following sections, you'll learn how to retrieve information for the most common objects in your infrastructure, such as machines, Delivery Controllers, catalogs, and applications.

# The Get-BrokerMachine cmdlet

In a Citrix infrastructure, broker machines are servers or desktops that deliver resources to users. For example, the worker servers that publish applications in a XenApp site are considered as broker machines.

Using the Get-BrokerMachine cmdlet, you can obtain objects that represent the broker machines in your infrastructure. If you run it without any parameter, you get the full list of broker machines and their attributes.

You can select the attributes to be retrieved using the -Property parameter. For example, if you want to display only the MachineName and CatalogName attributes, you can use the following command:

```
PS C:\> Get-BrokerMachine -Property MachineName,CatalogName
```

This command will display the output shown in the following screenshot:

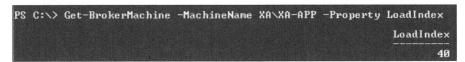
```
PS C:\> Get-BrokerMachine -Property MachineName,CatalogName

MachineName                                    CatalogName
-----------                                    -----------
XA\XA-APP                                      StaticServers
XA\XA-WORKER01                                 MCSCatalog
XA\XA-WORKER02                                 MCSCatalog
XA\XA-WORKER03                                 MCSCatalog
```

Displaying only a subset of attributes

You can also filter the results by searching only for objects with attributes that match the values you specify. A typical script I use to monitor the load of a worker server is as follows:

```
PS C:\> Get-BrokerMachine -MachineName <myServer> -Property LoadIndex
```

This command will display the output shown in the following screenshot:

```
PS C:\> Get-BrokerMachine -MachineName XA\XA-APP -Property LoadIndex
                                                          LoadIndex
                                                          ---------
                                                                 40
```

Retrieving the LoadIndex value of a broker machine

 Wildcard searches are supported for the DNSName, HostedMachineId, HostedMachineName, and MachineName parameters.

Other interesting attributes that you can monitor are shown in the following table:

| Attribute | Description |
| --- | --- |
| FaultState | This is the health state of the machine; the summary state of any current fault state of the machine. It can be in any one of the following states:<br><br>• None: The machine is healthy<br>• FailedToStart: The controller failed to start the machine<br>• StuckOnBoot: The machine did not boot correctly<br>• Unregistered: The machine has failed to register<br>• MaxCapacity: The machine has reached its full capacity |
| InMaintenanceMode | This shows that the machine is set in maintenance mode. |

| Attribute | Description |
|---|---|
| RegistrationState | The registration state can be Unregistered, Initializing, Registered, or AgentError. |
| SessionCount | This shows the number of active sessions on the machine. |
| SessionsPending | This is the number of pending (brokered, but not yet established) sessions on the machine. For multisession machines, this also includes established sessions that have not yet completed their logon processing. |

# The Get-BrokerController cmdlet

Delivery Controllers are retrieved through the Get-BrokerController cmdlet. The BrokerController object represents a single instance of a controller running instances of the Broker Service. The most important property to monitor purposes is the controller's State property, which can assume the values Active, Failed, On, and Off.

# The Get-BrokerCatalog cmdlet

Catalogs are groups of related physical or virtual machines that have been configured on the site. The Get-BrokerCatalog cmdlet returns BrokerCatalog objects.

I often used the following *Count attributes to monitor possible provisioning problems (for example, catalogs with no allocated machines):

| Attribute | Description |
|---|---|
| AssignedCount | This shows the number of assigned machines (machines that have been assigned to a user/users or a client's name/address) |
| AvailableAssignedCount | This shows the number of available machines (not in a group) that are also assigned to users |
| AvailableCount | This shows the number of available machines (those not in any group) |
| AvailableUnassignedCount | This shows the number of available machines (those not in any group) that are not assigned to users |
| UnassignedCount | This shows the number of unassigned machines (machines not assigned to users) |
| UsedCount | This shows the number of machines in the catalog that are in a group |

# The Get-BrokerApplicationInstance cmdlet

Using the Get-BrokerApplicationInstance cmdlet, you can obtain the instances of applications delivered by your infrastructure. They are the applications that are now running on desktops or servers. This can be useful to monitor the number of concurrent executions of the same application.

Only published applications that are launched from a Citrix client are returned.

 A different cmdlet, Get-BrokerApplication, is used to get the configuration of the applications that have been published.

If one application is launched more than once in the same session, the cmdlet returns a single object with a value greater than 1 for the Instances attribute, as shown in the following screenshot:

```
PS C:\> Get-BrokerApplicationInstance


ApplicationName : Notepad
ApplicationUid  : 1
Instances       : 2
MachineName     : XA\XA-APP
```

Running two copies of one application in the same session

# Counting objects

Several of my monitoring scripts count things such as the number of active Delivery Controllers, the number of available machines in catalogs, and so on.

Using PowerShell, it's easy to count the number of objects a cmdlet returns. Each array in PowerShell has a count property that returns the number of items it contains.

The problem is that sometimes cmdlets don't return an array. If the result is a single item (or no items at all), the result is a single object (or no object), and the count property is not available unless you force the result to be an array using the @ sign.

For example, if you have a single Delivery Controller in your infrastructure, the following command does not return anything:

```
PS C:\> (Get-BrokerController).count
PS C:\>
```

However, if you add the @ sign before the cmdlet, it works:

```
PS C:\> @(Get-BrokerController).count
1
PS C:\>
```

 With PowerShell v3, the use of the @ sign is unnecessary. When asked for the count property, it automatically checks whether the object is an array or not.

# Citrix® Director

With XenApp 7.5, Citrix unified all the monitoring and troubleshooting tools in a single product called the Citrix Director.

Director is a web-based tool that enables system administrators to perform the following tasks:

- Monitor a XenApp or XenDesktop environment
- Troubleshoot issues
- Perform support tasks for end users

## System requirements

Director requires 50 MB of disk space, Microsoft .NET Framework 4.5, and IIS (Internet Information Services) 7.0 with ASP.NET 2.0.

The minimum hardware requirements are as follows:

- A CPU with four cores
- 4 GB of RAM memory

Director supports the Windows 2008 R2 Service Pack 1, Windows 2012, and Windows 2012 R2 operating systems.

 Director can be accessed using Internet Explorer 9 or later, Mozilla Firefox, or Google Chrome.

The latest release of Citrix Director is not compatible with XenApp deployments earlier than Version 7.5 or XenDesktop deployments earlier than Version 7.

# Installation

Director can be installed on one of the Delivery Controllers in your site or on a dedicated server.

 When Director is used in an infrastructure with more than one site, be sure that all the servers have a synchronized system clock (for example, use NTP); otherwise, the sites might not be displayed correctly in Director.

The installer looks for prerequisites and installs all missing components (for example, the .NET Framework). It also sets up the IIS web server and performs the initial configuration.

If Director is installed on a Delivery Controller, the installer automatically configures it to communicate with the local controller configuring `localhost` as the server address. If, on the contrary, you're installing Director on a dedicated server, you're prompted to the **Fully-Qualified Domain Name (FQDN)** of a controller of your site.

Director does not load balance between controllers; it discovers all other controllers and falls back to other controllers if the controller you specified fails.

After the installation, Citrix Director is available at `http://<server_FQDN>/Director`.

The Citrix login page is shown in the following screenshot:

Citrix Director login page

Even if Director does not strictly require it, my suggestion is to implement SSL (HTTPS) on the IIS website (and configure IIS to require it) that hosts Director to secure the communication between the browser and the server.

You might also want to set Director as the default page in IIS (so that users don't need to remember and type the full URL), and prepopulate the list of available Active Directory domains instead of asking users to type the name of the domain they belong to.

# Director and EdgeSight®

In the past, system administrators used Citrix Desktop Director for day-to-day management, helpdesk support for XenDesktop infrastructures, and Citrix EdgeSight for full-time monitoring of both XenApp and XenDesktop environments.

With XenApp 7.5, the two products have been expanded and combined into a single architecture, as shown in the following screenshot:

Director and EdgeSight are now available from a single web console

After the log in, Citrix Director opens the Troubleshooting Dashboard, which provides real-time assessment of the site. Using this dashboard, administrators are able to see health, usage, and performance data updated every minute.

The gray panels at the top highlight failures in desktops, servers, or user connections; each panel will automatically slide down if any error is detected.

The two charts in the middle display the actual number of sessions and the average logon durations, both significant values that might help prevent and resolve issues prior to a major impact to the user experience.

The infrastructure panel at the bottom provides infrastructure health alerts.

The dashboard presents the last 60 minutes. Administrators can click on **Trends** to view historical trends and export the data into a CSV (comma-separated value) file, or export the chart into a PDF file.

From the troubleshooting dashboard, administrators can click on the failure or sessions number; the **Filters** view is automatically opened. In this table view, administrators can easily discover the machines that have been affected by the failure and the reason and time of failure. More than one row can be selected at a time, allowing global actions to quickly remediate the issue.

Citrix EdgeSight, when integrated in Director, provides the following two key features:

- Performance management
- Network analysis

With performance management, administrators can create trend reports for both capacity and health. For example, you can create a report to compare the number of logged users to the logon duration, or you can compare the load on the infrastructure during different months.

Director also offers an auto-baselining feature that can analyze the performance data and understand what normal behavior is. You can then compare a data range to this baseline to verify whether any changes to the infrastructure (for example, the delivery of a new application) affected the overall performance.

Network analysis is a new reporting tool that leverages NetScaler HDX Insight. With this tool, Citrix administrators can have a deeper network visibility. They can diagnose whether a performance problem (a user calls complaining that applications are slow) is due to a high latency or a low bandwidth connection. Moreover, they can understand if this problem affects many users or it's isolated to one single user.

Depending on your license, some of the following features of Citrix Director might be available:

- All the editions include Director for real-time monitoring and troubleshooting (up to 7 days of data)
- XenApp Platinum adds EdgeSight performance management features and historical monitoring (up to a full year of data)
- XenApp Platinum and NetScaler Enterprise add EdgeSight network analysis (60 minutes of network data)
- XenApp Platinum and NetScaler Platinum add EdgeSight network analysis (unlimited network data)

# Roles and helpdesk console

Both Citrix Studio and Citrix Director offer a delegated administration model.

This model uses the following three concepts:

- **Administrators**: They are individual persons or groups identified by Active Directory accounts
- **Roles**: They are job functions that have defined permissions associated with them (for example, creating a delivery group)
- **Scopes**: They are collections of objects

Using the three preceding concepts, you can define who (the administrator) can perform what (the role) on which items (the scope).

Using Citrix Studio (**Configuration | Administrators**), you can add new administrators, scopes, and roles, or you can change the existing ones, as shown in the following screenshot:

Configuring a delegated administration in Citrix Studio

If a user with the **Help Desk Administrator** role logs in to Director, a dedicated dashboard is presented. This dashboard is designed to help the operator to troubleshoot end user issues in the following ways:

- The operator is prompted to the account of the user who's reporting an issue
- After having searched for the user, the operator is moved to the **Activity Manager** console where he/she can view and terminate the applications and processes the user is running, log off the user, or shadow the connection, as shown in the following screenshot:

## Monitoring virtual infrastructure

If your Citrix environment is running on a virtual infrastructure, the hypervisor might cause performance issues, or a physical host might experience problems that could affect the virtual machines running on that host.

Director can monitor the virtual environment for alerts and display them in its dashboard; system administrators can then quickly assess whether the issue is a host-related issue, without the need to open the hypervisor's management console.

 At the moment, Director can display alerts for Citrix XenServer and VMware vSphere, but not for Microsoft Hyper-V.

Hypervisor alerts are shown under the **Infrastructure** panel, as shown in the following screenshot:

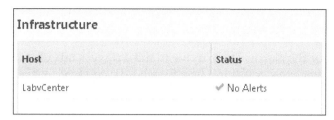

Director monitors the virtual infrastructure

The hypervisor alert is enabled by configuring alerts in its management console. The different kinds of alerts that Director can receive are the following:

- CPU usage alert
- Memory usage alert
- Network usage alert
- Storage throughput alert

To configure an alert for a XenServer host, open XenCenter and right-click on the host you want to configure the alert for (for storage throughput alerts, select a storage repository).

Select **Properties** from the drop-down menu and click on **Alerts**.

Select the checkbox next to the alert you wish to enable, and configure the threshold and the amount of time the threshold has to be breached for before the alert is raised.

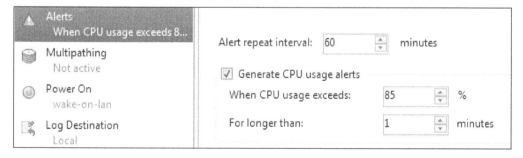

Enabling alerts in XenServer

In a vSphere environment, open the vSphere client, navigate to **Inventory | Hosts and Clusters**, and right-click on the host you want to configure the alert for (for storage throughput alerts, select a data store from **Datastores and Datastore Clusters**).

Navigate to **Alarm | Add Alarm...** from the drop-down menu.

Provide a name for the alarm. Then, move to the **Triggers** tab, click on **Add**, and configure the trigger type, condition (the threshold), and length (the amount of time before the alert is raised), as shown in the following screenshot:

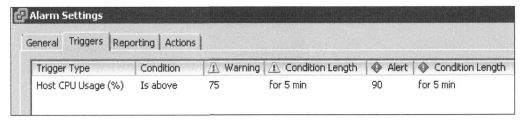

Enabling alerts in vSphere

The supported trigger types are as follows:

- **Host CPU Usage (%)**
- **Host Disk Usage (KBps)**
- **Host Memory Usage (%)**
- **Host Network Usage (kbps)**

# The Monitor Service Open Data API

In addition to using the Citrix Director console, historical data is available by querying the Monitor Service using the **Open Data** (**OData**) protocol (http://www.odata.org).

Using the OData API, you can get information about objects such as hypervisors, machines, desktop groups, users, sessions, and connections.

The following two endpoints are exposed by the Delivery Controller server:

- The Methods endpoint (used by the Director): http://<dc-server>/ Citrix/Monitor/OData/v1/Methods
- The Data endpoint (with read-only access and support for the OData query language): http://<dc-server>/Citrix/Monitor/OData/v1/Data

Before being able to retrieve the data, you must authenticate with a valid account. The data you can access is determined by XenApp roles and permissions.

## Using Excel PowerPivot

PowerPivot is a free plugin for Excel; you can download it from Microsoft's website.

After having installed it, open Excel and click on the **PowerPivot** tab, and then click on **From Data Feeds** in the ribbon.

Choose a connection name and enter the data endpoint of your Delivery Catalog as **Data Feed Url**. Select the tables you want to import into Excel and click on **Finish**, as shown in the following screenshot:

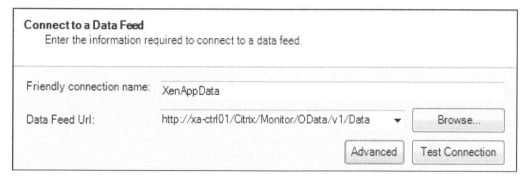

Using Excel PowerPivot to get data from Monitor Service

# Optimizing the infrastructure

With the help of the monitoring tools previously listed, a system administrator can quickly detect performance issues or infrastructure problems. In this section, I will explain some advanced features and configurations that can be used to resolve these issues and optimize the overall performance.

# CPU and memory optimizations

Worker servers can host many concurrent user sessions and applications. These sessions typically consume CPU and memory resources.

A critical aspect is how the operating system distributes the resources across the different sessions. For example, consider a user who is using a spreadsheet to perform complex financial calculations; his session can consume most of the CPU resources available on the server, potentially slowing down the work of other connected users.

XenApp 6.5 offered an internal feature named CPU Utilization Management to optimize CPU allocation. With XenApp 7.5, this feature is no longer available because the latest versions of Windows Server (2008 and 2012) include a similar feature, Windows **Dynamic Fair Share Scheduling (DFSS)**.

> If you implemented CPU Utilization Management in XenApp 6.5, you probably disabled Windows DFSS since the two features cannot work together.

## Windows Dynamic Fair Share Scheduling

Windows DFSS is the CPU optimization solution Microsoft included in Remote Desktop Services since Windows 2008 R2.

DFSS uses the kernel-level scheduling mechanism of Windows to distribute processor time across sessions, ensuring that each one does not consume too many resources and does not degrade the performances of the others.

Windows 2012 extended the power of DFSS, adding the ability to control network and disk resources, just as the load is distributed equally across the sessions running on the servers for the CPU. The goal of DFSS remains to prevent excessive resource usage by one user and provide all users with the same experience; fair share techniques do not ensure that resources are not exhausted.

Working with a kernel driver (`tsfairshare.sys`) allows DFSS to react instantly when a new session is launched (Citrix CPU Utilization Management acted upon triggers or on a scheduled basis).

DFSS is enabled by default on both Windows 2008 R2 and Windows 2012. It can be disabled, but I strongly suggest letting it be enabled via **Group Policy**, as shown in the following screenshot:

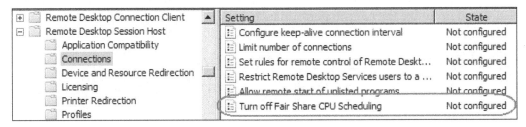

Disabling Fair Share CPU Scheduling

[  At the moment, you can't disable fair sharing of network and disk resources in Windows 2012. ]

The default behavior of DFSS is to distribute the resources equally across the sessions; you can change this using **Windows System Resource Manager (WSRM)**.

This tool is available as a feature you can install from Windows Server Manager and requires Windows Internal Database (automatically installed).

To manage the resources on your server, you can apply one of the five built-in resource allocation policies, or you can create a new policy combining process-matching criteria and existing resource allocation policies; only one resource allocation policy can be used at a time to manage a computer.

I found a very useful **Weighted_Remote_Sessions** built-in policy. With this policy, you can categorize users and groups into basic, standard, and premium workloads to appropriately prioritize resources, as shown in the following screenshot:

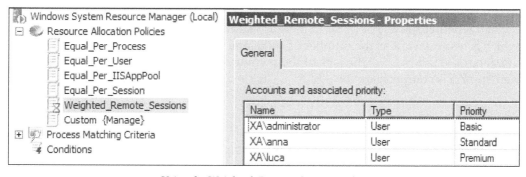

Using the Weighted_Remote_Sessions policy

When you install WSRM on Windows 2012, you're warned that this tool is *deprecated*. This version still includes the tool and it works fine, but the next server release will not have this tool. At the moment, it's not clear whether Microsoft is planning to replace it with a new version or completely change the DFSS feature.

# Memory optimization

In XenApp 6.5, you can enable memory optimization, a feature that optimizes memory usage by relocating **Dynamic Link Libraries (DLLs)** to avoid collisions.

A DLL is a library that contains code, data, and resources; it can be used by different programs at the same time. By using DLLs, applications can be modularized and can include third-party libraries. DLLs promote code reuse and reduce the load time of the program because they are loaded into memory when requested.

Every DLL has a preferred base address, which is the memory address where the module should be mapped into the process' address space (virtual memory) by the operating system.

If two DLLs have the same preferred base address, a collision occurs and the OS has to relocate the DLL to a different available address when the OS loads them into memory. A relocated DLL cannot be shared by different applications.

This feature is not available in XenApp 7.5. From Windows 2008 R2 (and Windows 7 for desktop OSes) onwards, Microsoft introduced a new feature called **Address Space Load Randomization** (**ASLR**), which makes memory optimization impossible to implement.

In earlier versions of Windows, common system components were loaded at fixed locations. This meant that malware and virus authors could use buffer overruns because they knew the exact memory addresses of those components. With ASLR, the memory manager picks a random base address from one of the 256 available locations during the boot process, and DLLs are loaded in a memory address computed by adding the random base address to their preferred address.

I tested whether the use of random memory addresses renders DLL rebasing, which is less relevant as the number of collisions is reduced compared to the earlier versions of Windows. So, the lack of the memory optimization feature in the new XenApp 7.5 is compensated by ASLR.

# Network optimization

If the published applications generate high traffic on your network (for example, accessing network shares or databases), you may experience high response time and, worse, high CPU load time because the CPU is busy processing network packets.

Windows 2008 and 2012 offer some advanced features to offload some of the CPU activity to the network adapter and distribute processing across multiple processor cores.

 On a virtual environment, make sure you're using a supported virtual network card, and install its driver in the guest operating system. On VMware vSphere, most of the advanced features are supported by using the VMXNET3 adapter and a virtual hardware of Version 7 or higher.

# Power plan

By default, Windows is configured with a **Balanced** power plan. Changing it to **High performance** (by navigating to **Control Panel | Power Options**) can increase the overall performance of the server, including the network subsystem, as shown in the following screenshot:

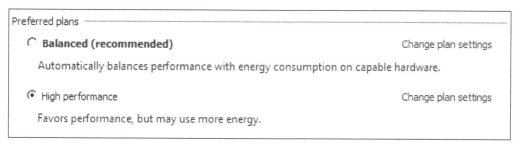

Choosing the High performance power plan

# TCP Chimney Offload

TCP Chimney Offload is a networking technology that helps transfer workload from the CPU to a network adapter during network data transfer.

It can be enabled in the following two locations:

- The operating system, using the `netsh int tcp set global chimney=enabled` command
- The **Advanced** properties page of the network adapter

TCP Chimney Offload will work only if enabled in both the locations.

You can verify that Windows is offloading the connections using the `netstat -t` command and analyzing the `Offload State` (`InHost` or `Offloaded`) column, as shown in the following screenshot:

Using netstat to determine if a connection has been offloaded

## Receive Side Scaling

**Receive Side Scaling (RSS)** is a Windows feature that enables network adapters to distribute the kernel-mode network processing load across multiple processor cores in multicore computers. It was introduced in Windows 2003 and enhanced in Windows 2012, providing automatic load balancing capabilities for non-TCP traffic.

You can determine the current status of RSS using the following command:

```
C:\>netsh int tcp show global
```

To enable or disable RSS, type the following commands:

```
C:\>netsh int tcp set global rss=enabled
C:\>netsh int tcp set global rss=disabled
```

# Load balancing and failover

One of the most radical changes the adoption of **FlexCast Management Architecture (FMA)** brought into XenApp 7.5 is in the way resources are delivered to users. Zones, worker groups, load balancing policies, and so on have all been (partially) replaced by new concepts and configurations.

 A configuration that's no longer available in XenApp 7.5 is the possibility to limit the number of concurrent executions (instances) of an application.

# Machine catalogs and delivery groups

A machine catalog is a collection of identical machines running either a Windows desktop OS or a Windows server OS, with the Delivery Agent installed.

The machines in a catalog can be provisioned through **Machine Catalog Services (MCS)** or provisioning services, or they can be manually created and added. In *Chapter 1, Designing the New FlexCast® Management Architecture*, you learned how to configure a dynamic machine catalog with machines managed by MCS.

A delivery group is created to deliver desktops or applications. It's a flexible way of allocating machines and applications from a machine catalog to users.

A delivery group can contain machines from multiple catalogs, but a machine can belong to a single machine catalog, as shown in the following diagram:

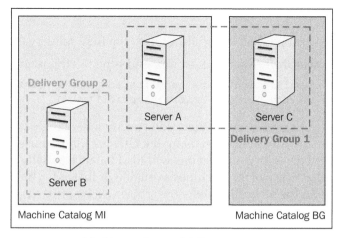

Machine catalogs and delivery groups

# Load balancing

When you create a new delivery group in the Studio console, you can only choose a single machine catalog.

After having created the delivery group, use the **Add machines...** action to choose a different catalog and add machines from it.

 Using PowerShell, you can create an empty delivery group with `New-BrokerDesktopGroup` and add machines with `Add-BrokerMachinesToDesktopGroup`.

In XenApp 7.5, there's no concept of a load balancing policy. So, you can't assign any kind of priority to the machines assigned to a delivery group.

# Failover

Since assigning multiple catalogs to a delivery group in the previous section does not allow configuring any kind of priority to be set, you need to create a second delivery group if you want to provide failover with preference.

Having created the two machine catalogs and delivery groups, you can publish the applications; however, you can only publish applications to a single delivery group using the Studio console. You can, of course, publish the same application to different delivery groups, but you'll end up with a copy (**Application** and **Application_1**), and, worse, your users will receive two icons.

Again, Windows PowerShell can help if you perform the following steps:

- Use Studio and publish the application to the first delivery group.
- Open a PowerShell command prompt and type the following command:

```
Add-BrokerApplication -Name <application_name> -DesktopGroup
<second_delivery_group> -Priority <priority>
```

The `Add-BrokerApplication` cmdlet lets you specify a `Priority` value (the default priority when you add an application using the GUI is `0`). If you use the same value for the two delivery groups, your sessions will load balance equally between them and fail over if either one has no machines available. If instead, a delivery group has a lower priority than the other, that delivery group will be utilized only if there are no available machines in the one with higher priority.

The two delivery groups are also visible in the application properties, as shown in the following screenshot:

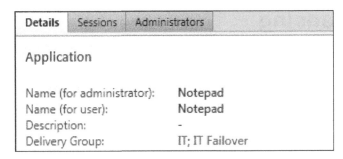

Two delivery groups configured for an application

 Priority values are visible only using PowerShell, as shown in the following command:
```
C:\>Get-BrokerApplication -Name "Notepad"
Application Type:           HostedOnDesktop
AssociatedDesktopGroupPriorities    {0, 2}
```

# Load Management

Load Management, not to be confused with load balancing, is the way Citrix XenApp determines how server load is calculated. It is designed to indicate how suitable a worker server is to receive a new user session.

A server's load index might be the aggregate of the following components:

- Computer performance counter-based metrics such as CPU, memory, and disk usage
- Session count

As only the Delivery Controller can determine the session load, a server's overall load index is calculated on the Delivery Controller and not the Virtual Delivery Agent.

Different XenApp policies can be applied to the worker servers to configure the weight each counter value has when the Load Management tool calculates the load index, as shown in the following screenshot:

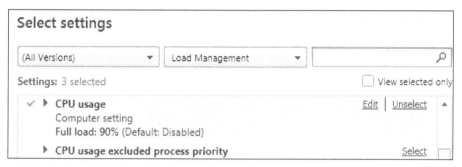

Load Management settings

 You cannot apply Load Management policies to specific applications such as XenApp 6.5; you can create load evaluators and apply them to applications.

The Load Management policy settings are as follows:

- **CPU, Memory, Disk usage**: This specifies if CPU, memory, and disk usage are included or excluded from load calculations and the value at which the server reports a full load
- **CPU usage excluded process priority**: This specifies the priority level at which a process' CPU usage is excluded from the CPU usage load index
- **Memory usage base load**: This specifies the memory usage below which the server is considered to have zero load (it's an estimation of the operating system's memory usage)
- **Concurrent logon tolerance**: This specifies the maximum number of concurrent logons the server can accept
- **Maximum number of sessions**: This specifies the maximum number of concurrent sessions the server can host

In Director, the load evaluator index is shown in comparison to the number of connected users. Moving the mouse over each data point shows a detailed panel with the percentage of the different load values, as shown in the following screenshot:

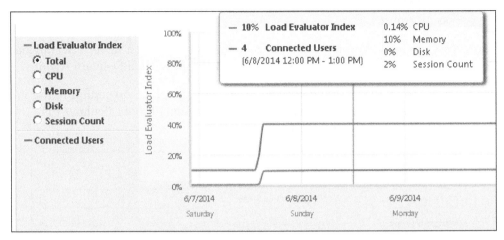

Viewing Load Evaluator Index in Director

# Zone versus site

In XenApp 6.5, a system administrator designing an infrastructure that will be distributed between various locations, or even countries, can logically divide a single farm into zones.

With FMA, there's no zone replacement; you need to create an individual XenApp site for every former zone and use StoreFront to aggregate or failover applications delivered from each site.

 If you have low latency connections between the different datacenters, you can consider stretching a single XenApp 7.5 site across them, thus avoiding installing in each datacenter Delivery Controller, Database Server, and so on.

# StoreFront configuration

Unfortunately, configuring StoreFront to load balance and failover functionalities cannot be done using the graphical interface but must be performed by changing the configuration files.

An XML editor (for example, Notepad++) and the PsGetSid utility included in SysInternals PsTools (`http://download.sysinternals.com/files/PSTools.zip`) can help during the configuration.

Open the `web.config` file in `C:\inetpub\wwwroot\Citrix\storename` and locate the `<resourcesWingConfigurations>` node, as shown in the following screenshot:

```
web - Notepad                                                            _ □ X
File  Edit  Format  View  Help
      <resourcesCommon>
        <resourcesWingConfigurations>
          <resourcesWingConfiguration name="Default" wingName="Default" />
        </resourcesWingConfigurations>
      </resourcesCommon>
```

Configuring StoreFront's web.config file

The configuration requires the following elements:

- `userFarmMapping`: This specifies the groups of deployments and defines the load balancing and failover behavior between them
- `groups`: This defines the Active Directory groups (name and SID; use PsGetSid to get it)
- `equivalentFarmSet`: This specifies a group of equivalent deployments; with the `loadBalanceMode` attribute, you can define whether users are randomly assigned to the deployments (`LoadBalanced`) or whether users are connected to the first available deployment (`Failover`)
- `primaryFarmRefs`: This defines the primary deployments in the farm set (enter the exact names of deployments that you have already added to the store)
- `backupFarmRefs`: This defines the backup deployments in the farm set

Configuring StoreFront for high availability can be difficult; remember to back up the original `web.config` file and follow the Citrix documentation (`http://support.citrix.com/proddocs/topic/dws-storefront-25/dws-plan-ha.html`), where you can find several configuration examples.

# Summary

In this chapter, you learned how to monitor your XenApp infrastructure.

Performance counters can provide you with real-time and historical data, and you can get the health status of all the components in your infrastructure using PowerShell. Using the OData API, you can access performance data from any OData consumer.

Citrix Director is the new, powerful tool included in XenApp 7.5 that helps system administrators and help-desk operators to identify and resolve problems affecting performance and end user experience.

Some of the advanced features included in XenApp 6.5 to optimize the usage of CPU and memory are not available in the new version, but they are somehow replaced by the Windows features.

Using a mix of delivery groups, Load Management policies, and advanced StoreFront configurations, you can improve how applications and sessions are balanced on your servers.

In the next chapter, you'll learn how to monitor and optimize the end user experience.

# 3
# Monitor and Optimize End User Experience

The most frequent complaint that system administrators receive from users about XenApp is definitely about the applications starting slowly. They certainly do not consider the fact that, at least for the first time, when you launch an application published by XenApp, an entire login process takes place.

The use of mobile devices and/or mobile connections is becoming more and more frequent. This introduces new problems such as network interruptions and same application (even multimedia ones) usage on different devices with different CPU power and screen sizes.

In this chapter, you'll learn about the following topics:

- Steps forming the login process, the systems involved, and how to monitor and optimize the duration of each step
- Features available to maintain user sessions during network interruptions or when the user moves from one device to another
- Optimizing printing and multimedia applications
- Leveraging AppDNA to test application compatibility in different scenarios and environments

# The logon process

The following diagram explains the logon process, which starts when a user logs in to the StoreFront server and concludes when the requested application is started. It illustrates a typical local login without including the use of a NetScaler Gateway.

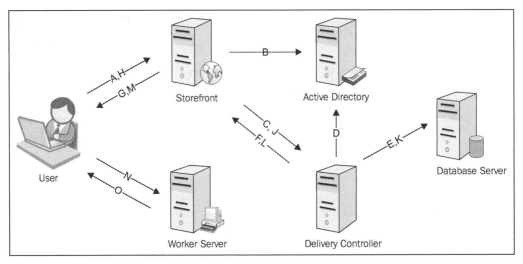

The logon process

# Enumeration

A user enters the username and password in the web login form of the StoreFront server (**A**). The authentication service running on StoreFront validates the credentials with a **Domain Controller** (**DC**) (**B**) and fetches all the user group memberships. StoreFront checks its local database (datastore) for existing user subscriptions, and it validates the user mapping configuration in a multisite configuration to determine the site that the user belongs to (as explained in *Chapter 2, Monitor and Optimize Infrastructure – Director and EdgeSight®*).

StoreFront forwards the credentials to one of the Delivery Controllers of that site (**C**).

 If the user is not a member of a configured group, StoreFront will send the request to all the sites that have been added to the store.

The Delivery Controller validates the credentials against Active Directory (**D**) and, once validated, identifies a list of available resources by querying the SQL Database (**E**).

The list is sent to the StoreFront server (**F**), which displays them—including the existing subscriptions—in a web page (**G**).

# Execution

The user clicks on an icon in order to request a resource (**H**). The request is forwarded to the Delivery Controller (**J**), which queries the SQL database to determine the best host (worker server) to fulfill the request (**K**).

The Delivery Controller sends the connection information to StoreFront (**L**), which creates a launch (`.ica`) file that is sent to the user (**M**).

Citrix Receiver, which runs on the user's device, receives the launch file and makes a connection to the worker server (**N**), which executes the requested application (**O**).

# Session setup

When the worker server is requested for a resource, and the user does not have an existing session, the Delivery Agent validates that a Citrix license is available and then creates a new Windows session.

A number of steps are performed by the operating system, which are as follows:

1. It checks whether a **Remote Desktop Services Client Access License** (**RDS CAL**) is available.

2. It authenticates the user against Active Directory and, if successful, queries for account details such as **Group Policy Objects** (**GPOs**), profile location, and so on.

3. It applies the policies (including Citrix ones), executes all applications included in the **Startup** menu, and finally launches the application.

# Analyzing the logon process

Users perceive the overall duration of the process from the time when they click on the icon to the appearance of the application on their desktops. To troubleshoot slowness, a system administrator must know the duration of the individual steps.

Citrix Director allows system administrators and helpdesk operators to examine the average logon duration and inspect the time it took for a given user to log on to the current session. They can inspect in the following ways:

- The average logon duration chart is visible in the main dashboard, and it's also available in the **Logon Performance** tab of **Historical Trends**.

- To display the logon duration data for a single user, search the user and click on **Details** on the top right of the user's **Activity Manager** page. The panel updates about every 3 minutes.

The logon process is divided into seven phases:

| Phase | Description |
| --- | --- |
| Brokering | Time taken to decide which worker server will be used to run the requested application |
| VM start | Time taken to boot the desktop (not applicable for XenApp) |
| HDX connection | Time taken for **High Definition eXperience** (**HDX**) connection establishment |
| Authentication | Time taken to authenticate the user |
| GPOs | Time taken to apply Windows GPOs |
| Login scripts | Time taken to execute login scripts |
| Profile load | Time taken to load the user profile |
| Interactive session | Time taken to create the user session |

If you move the mouse pointer over the chart, a pop-up dialog is shown with the duration of each phase, as shown in the following screenshot:

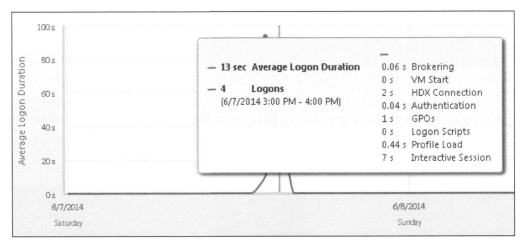

The phases of the logon process

The total logon time is not an exact sum of these phases. Some phases occur in parallel, and additional processing checks occur in some phases.

 To identify the phase that could cause abnormal logon duration, compare the amount of time taken in each phase with the average duration for the user over the last 7 days.

# Optimizing the logon process

Using Director, you can now easily determine the phases where most of the time is spent. From my experience, slowness in the logon process is often caused by the following issues:

- Authentication issues
- Profile issues
- GPO and logon script issues

In the following sections, you'll learn how to mitigate these issues.

## Authentication issues

During the logon process, authentication happens at multiple steps. Citrix XenApp integrates with Active Directory, and the authentication is, therefore, performed by a DC server of your domain.

Slowness in the DC response, caused by an overloaded server, can slow down the entire process. Worse, if the DC is unavailable, a domain member server might try to connect for 30 seconds before timing out and choosing a different DC.

Domain member servers choose the DC to authenticate users based on their membership to Active Directory sites. If sites are not correctly configured or don't reflect the real topology of your network, a domain member server might decide to use a remote DC through a slow WAN link instead of using a DC on the same LAN. For more details on Active Directory topology, refer to the Microsoft AD DS Design Guide (http://technet.microsoft.com/en-us/library/cc772013(v=ws.10).aspx).

# Profile issues

Each user has a profile that is a collection of personal files and settings. Windows offers different type of profiles, with advantages and disadvantages, as shown in the following table:

| Type | Description |
| --- | --- |
| Local | The profile folder is local to each server |
| Roaming | The profile folder is saved on a central storage (usually a file server) |
| Mandatory | A read-only profile is assigned to users; changes are not saved across sessions |

From the administrator's point of view, mandatory profiles are the best option because they are simple to maintain, they allow users to log on quickly, and they can't modify Windows or application settings. This option, however, is not often feasible. I could use mandatory profiles only in specific cases; for example, when users have to run only a single application without the need to customize it.

Local profiles are almost never used in a XenApp environment because even if they offer the fastest logon time, they are not consistent across servers and sessions. Furthermore, you'll end up with all your worker servers storing local profiles for all your users, and this is a waste of disk space.

System administrators usually choose roaming profiles for their users. Roaming profiles indeed allow consistency across servers and sessions and preserve user settings and changes.

Roaming profiles are, however, the most significant cause of slow logons; if not monitored regularly, they can rapidly grow to a large size. A small profile with a large number of files, for example, a profile with many cookies, can cause delays too.

Roaming profiles also suffer from the last write wins problem. In a distributed environment such as a XenApp site, it is not unlikely that users are connected to different servers at the same time. Profiles are updated when users log off. So, with different sessions on different servers, some settings can be overwritten or, worse, the profile can be corrupted.

Later in this chapter, I'll introduce Citrix Profile Management, which offers the same advantages of roaming profiles, but it solves some of the preceding problems.

# GPO and logon script issues

In a Windows environment, it's common to apply settings and customizations via GPOs or by using logon scripts.

Numerous GPOs and long-running scripts can significantly impact the speed of the logon process. The following are some of the best practices when working with GPOs and logon scripts:

- **Reduce the number of GPOs by merging them when possible**: The time Windows takes to apply 10 GPOs is much more than the time to apply a single GPO with all its settings

- **Disable unused GPO sections**: It's common to have GPOs with only computer or user settings, explicitly disabling the unused section that can speed up the time required to apply them

- **Use GPOs instead of logon scripts**: Windows 2008 introduced Group Policy preferences, which can be used to perform common tasks (map network drives, change registry keys, and so on) previously performed by logon scripts

- **Assign logon scripts to users via GPOs**: We can assign logon scripts to users via GPOs rather than through the user account property settings

- **Be careful when configuring Internet Explorer via GPO**: It might add a 20 second delay to the logon process (some hotfixes are available, for example, http://support.microsoft.com/kb/941158)

# Citrix® Profile Management

Citrix Profile Management is a software component that provides an easy and reliable way to manage user profiles in Windows environments. It was developed to solve some of the well-known problems of Windows roaming profiles and provide users with faster logons and logoffs.

 Some third-party profile management solutions such as RES Workspace Manager, AppSense, and so on are available. A good comparison is available in the User Environment Management Smackdown whitepaper (http://www.pqr.com/user-environment-management-smackdown).

XenApp 7.5 includes the new Version 5.0 of Citrix Profile Management, and it is installed by default when you install the Virtual Delivery Agent, as shown in the following screenshot:

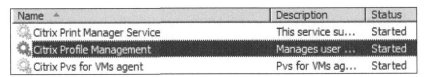

| Name ▲ | Description | Status |
|---|---|---|
| Citrix Print Manager Service | This service su... | Started |
| Citrix Profile Management | Manages user ... | Started |
| Citrix Pvs for VMs agent | Pvs for VMs ag... | Started |

Citrix Profile Management service is automatically installed with the Delivery Agent

The main features of Citrix Profile Management are as follows:

- Support for multiple sessions without the last write wins problem
- Ability to manage large profiles without the need to perform a full sync when the user logs on
- Support for v1 (Windows XP/2003) and v2 (Windows Vista/7/2008) profiles
- Ability to define inclusion/exclusion lists
- Extended synchronization, which can include files and folders external to the profile to support legacy applications
- Automatic configuration (only when used with XenDesktop)
- Configurable using Citrix policies (prior to Version 5.0, you had to use Windows GPOs)

**Profiles priority order**

If you deploy Citrix Profile Management, it takes precedence over any other profile assignment method. The priority order on a XenApp server is the following:

- Citrix Profile Management
- Remote Desktop Services profile assigned by a GPO
- Remote Desktop Services profile assigned by a user property
- Roaming profile assigned by a GPO
- Roaming profile assigned by a user property

# Folder Redirection

To reduce profile size and load time, you can redirect most of the user folders to a different location. Instead of saving files in the user's profile, you can store user data on network shares with Folder Redirection.

Folder Redirection does not require Citrix Profile Management. You can choose to let Windows manage user profiles (or install a third-party tool) and still redirect folders.

Folder Redirection is configured through Citrix policies (available under the **Folder Redirection** category). Most of the folders in a user profile can be redirected, including `Desktop`, `Downloads`, `Favorites`, `Music`, `Pictures`, and `Start Menu`.

For each folder, the following two policies are configurable:

- The path of the network share: This is the path of the network share that the folder will be redirected to.

- The settings of the redirection: Some folders can be redirected only to a UNC path while others can also be configured to follow the parent folder (for example, the `Music` folder can follow the `Document` folder). An example of redirecting the `Downloads` folder to a network share is shown in the following screenshot:

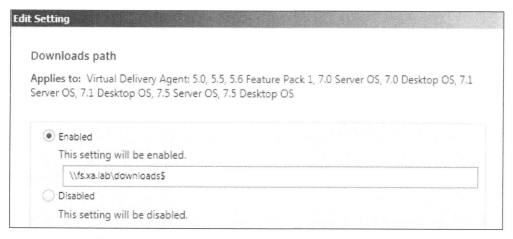

Creating a policy to redirect the Downloads folder to a network share

# Advanced redirection

The use of Citrix policies to configure Folder Redirection allows you to apply settings only to some of the delivery groups in your infrastructure. This is called advanced redirection.

In infrastructures using multiple operating systems (for example, when you deliver both desktops and applications), you might want some part of a user's profile to be shared by each OS. The rest of the profile is not shared and is used only by one OS. For example, you can decide to redirect the `Desktop` folder only when the user accesses a desktop virtual machine and not redirect it (to speed up the logon process) when the same user requests a published application.

> Citrix Profile Management prevents folders from being processed (exclusions). As the Folder Redirection and exclusion features work together, be sure not to exclude any redirected folder.

# Optimizing Storefront

When I moved from the old Web Interface to Storefront, I noticed that the latter was significantly slower than the former.

Storefront is a .NET application running on Microsoft IIS. Therefore, you can optimize the performance of Storefront by tuning the application server.

# Pooled sockets

The ability to maintain a pool of sockets instead of creating a new one each time a new user connects is already present in Citrix Web Interface. This gives a better performance, especially when using SSL.

To enable `pooledSockets`, open the `web.config` file in `C:\inetpub\wwwroot\Citrix\storename` and change `pooledSockets` to `on`, as shown in the following screenshot:

Enabling pooled sockets

# Application pool initialization

The default behavior of IIS is to initialize the application pool that runs Storefront when the first user connects. If the initialization process lasts a couple of minutes, and you're restarting the server every night, the first users arriving at the office in the morning will probably complain about slowness or timeouts when accessing the infrastructure.

Windows 2012 includes the **Application initialization** feature within the Web Server role. For Windows 2008 R2, you have to download it from the Microsoft website (`http://www.iis.net/downloads/microsoft/application-initialization`) and perform the following steps:

1. After installing the component and rebooting the server, open the `applicationHost.config` file located in `C:\Windows\System32\inetsrv\config`.

2. Locate the `<ApplicationPools>` node and add the `startMode="AlwaysRunning"` parameter on each application pool using a name starting with `Citrix`.

3. In the same file, locate the `<Sites>` node and add the `preloadEnabled="true"` parameter on each application corresponding to the application pools previously modified, as shown in the following screenshot:

```
<add name="Citrix Delivery Services Authentication" autoStart="true"
  managedRuntimeversion="v4.0" managedPipelineMode="Integrated"
  startMode="AlwaysRunning">  ⬅

<application path="/Citrix/Authentication"
  applicationPool="Citrix Delivery Services Authentication"
  preloadEnabled="true">  ⬅
```

Preloading Storefront application pools

4. Finally, you have to configure the initialization page for each site.

5. Open the `web.config` file contained in the folders in the following locations:

   ○ `C:\inetpub\wwwroot\Citrix\storename`

   ○ `C:\inetpub\wwwroot\Citrix\Authentication`

   ○ `C:\inetpub\wwwroot\Citrix\Roaming`

   ○ `C:\inetpub\wwwroot\AGServices`

6. Then, add the following code to these files in the `system.webserver` section:

```
<applicationInitialization skipManagedModules="true">
  <add initializationPage="/endpoints/v1"/>
</applicationInitialization>
```

7. Open the `web.config` file in `C:\inetpub\wwwroot\Citrix\storenameWeb`, and add the following code in the `system.webserver` section:

```
<applicationInitialization skipManagedModules="true">
  <add initializationPage="/Home/Index⊠ />
</applicationInitialization>
```

# Maintaining user sessions

Setting up a session is the most time-consuming task Citrix and Windows have to perform when a user requests an application. It's therefore important to keep an established user session even if a connectivity loss occurs. Users must be able to reconnect to your Citrix infrastructure and find all the applications still running.

Moreover, mobile users require the ability to roam quickly between devices. For example, consider a user working on a document using his tablet on the train while going to the office and, once there, wishing to continue his work on his personal computer.

Use the features explored in the following sections to optimize the reliability of sessions.

## Session Reliability

Session Reliability keeps sessions active on the user's screen during connectivity interruptions. Without Session Reliability, the session will be disconnected, applications will disappear from the user's device, and the user will have to reconnect to the infrastructure.

 With the previous versions of XenApp, I used to recommend disabling Session Reliability because it caused excessive network traffic and did not react very well to network interruptions. With XenApp 7.5, Citrix improved this feature and it is now very useful.

Three policy settings are available to configure Session Reliability, as shown in the following table:

| Setting | Description |
| --- | --- |
| Session reliability connections | Enable/disable Session Reliability |
| Session reliability port number | Set the TCP port (default 2598) for the incoming connections |
| Session reliability timeout | The time (in seconds) Session Reliability waits for a client to reconnect before disconnecting the session |

# Automatic client reconnection

When this feature is enabled, the Citrix Receiver attempts to reconnect the session automatically if it detects an unintended disconnection, until the reconnection is successful or the user cancels the attempts.

You can also define whether the user must reauthenticate after a reconnection or no authentication is required. In this case, a cookie is sent from the server to the client when the user logs in, and the client submits the same cookie to the server when reconnecting. User credentials are encrypted on the server side; the cookie contains the encryption key, so no credentials are stored on the client or sent during reconnection. The following screenshot displays this process:

Configuring auto client reconnect authentication

# ICA® Keep-Alive

The ICA Keep-Alive feature prevents broken connections from being disconnected. The server sends Keep-Alive packets every few seconds to detect whether the session is active, and the session is marked as disconnected only if a configurable timeout is reached.

ICA Keep-Alive does not work if Session Reliability is enabled; Session Reliability includes a different mechanism to send Keep-Alive messages.

# Workspace control

Workspace control lets desktops and applications follow a user from one device to another. This is a feature provided by Citrix StoreFront and enabled by default only for hosted applications.

If workspace control is enabled, when a user logs in, he or she is automatically reconnected to all running applications without the need to reopen them manually. A **Reconnect** button is presented to the user if automatic reconnection is disabled.

# Missing features

Some of the features that XenApp administrators used in the previous versions of XenApp are not available in XenApp 7.5 due to the adoption of FMA.

Session prelaunch and session lingering helped to anticipate the session setup (prelaunch) and improve the sharing of the same session between different applications (lingering).

On Citrix blogs (`http://blogs.citrix.com/2014/04/15/part-3-new-and-improved-session-pre-launch-and-lingering-coming-to-xenapp-and-xendesktop/`), it was announced that improved versions of the two features are under development and will be included in the future releases.

# Optimizing printing performance

With XenApp 6.5, Citrix introduced a new component, the Universal Print Server. This component eliminates the need to install numerous network printer drivers on XenApp worker servers, and it provides features such as image and font caching, advanced compression, optimization, and **Quality of Service (QoS)** support, which are not available in the Windows Print Provider.

To use the Universal Print Server, install it from the XenApp installation DVD on your printer servers and enable it via Citrix policies, as shown in the following screenshot:

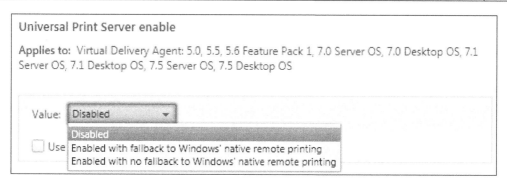

# Universal versus native printer driver

Citrix installs a universal printer driver, which supports the public device-independent settings defined by Microsoft. To optimize printing performance, Citrix suggests the use of both the Universal Print Server and the universal printer driver. Using Citrix policies, you can indeed configure printing quality, image compression, and optimizations, based on the available network bandwidth.

Sometimes, users need access to device settings that are specific to a printer driver manufacturer, and therefore, the specific driver must be used. The universal printer driver usage setting lets you decide whether the universal printer driver must always be used, it must be used only if a more specific driver is not available, or it must not be used at all.

# Improving user experience with Citrix® HDX™

HDX is more than a technology; it's a brand that encapsulates several different features, some of which were already available with different names.

## HDX™ MediaStream

HDX MediaStream is a set of features that are used to optimize the delivery of video/audio content. It offloads, when possible, the rendering of media content to the user device, reducing the server's CPU load and bandwidth usage. Since the media content is processed on the user's device, the playback is not affected by latency.

# Flash Redirection

Adobe Flash is a technology adopted in many websites, including YouTube and other video-hosting services. It's also used in some web applications, for example, the management console of VMware View.

You can configure HDX MediaStream to move the processing of Flash content from the published web browser to the end user device.

A second generation Flash Redirection is included with XenApp 7.5, and the new features are as follows:

- Support for user connections over WAN
- Intelligent Failback, which automatically detects when it's more efficient to render the Flash content on the server
- The URL Compatibility List that can help you define a list of URLs that should be rendered on the client or on the server, or be blocked

Flash Redirection is configured using the Citrix policy settings. On the user device, install Adobe Flash Player; no further configuration is required.

> Advanced configuration on the client is possible using the Flash Redirection - Client administrative template (HdxFlash-Client.adm) available in %Program Files%\Citrix\ICA Client\Configuration\language.

# Windows Media redirection

XenApp is able to send multimedia files to the client in the original, compressed format, and use the client's resources to decompress and render them. This feature is similar to the Flash Redirection feature introduced before, and it is also configurable with Citrix policies.

> If you enable **Windows Media client-side content fetching**, the end user device can stream multimedia files directly from the source website on the Internet or intranet rather than through the worker server. If the requirements for this client-side content fetching are not met, media delivery falls back to Windows Media redirection.

# Audio redirection

Today, it's very common to deliver unified communication applications such as Microsoft Lync via XenApp. Therefore, it's very important to provide high sound quality to users. XenApp offers several features and settings to optimize the audio quality and reduce bandwidth usage. You can use the **Audio quality** setting to configure the compression level of the audio stream to balance sound quality against overall session performance (for example, if you're using **Voice over IP (VoIP)** applications, you can choose **Medium - optimized for speech** to provide low latency, and at the same time, consume very low bandwidth). Another feature that dramatically reduces the latency is the ability to send and receive audio with UDP instead of tunneling the audio channel within the ICA connection. You can enable it with the **Audio over UDP Real-time Transport** setting. Remember that the client and the worker servers must be allowed to communicate through two configurable UDP ports.

If you don't need audio at all, you can completely disable the redirection of audio and microphone to save bandwidth.

> If you're using Microsoft Lync, you can leverage the HDX RealTime Optimization Pack for Microsoft Lync 2010 to optimize the performances of a Lync client in a XenApp or XenDesktop environment.

# HDX™ Mobile

XenApp 7.5 comes with a full set of features to optimize the user experience on mobile devices. The ICA protocol has been designed to traverse difficult network topologies such as 3G networks with high network variability and high latency.

These features often require no special configuration and are enabled by default. For example, HDX includes a native interface control channel that allows Windows apps to be refactored for a touch experience. A Mobile SDK is also provided for free on the Citrix website for developers willing to mobilize their applications.

# HDX™ Monitor

In XenApp 6.5, HDX Monitor was an external tool used to validate the operation and configuration of the HDX stack. With XenApp 7.5, it has been included in Director and is available on the user's **Details** page, as shown in the following screenshot:

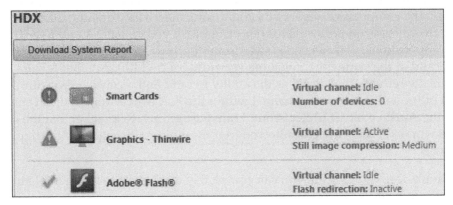

HDX Monitor within Citrix Director

HDX Monitor gives very good in-depth information about the actual user session, and it's very helpful for troubleshooting.

# Analyzing applications with AppDNA™

AppDNA is a Citrix tool that performs automated analysis of desktop and web applications to test their compatibility with different Windows platforms and web browsers.

It can be useful to accelerate the migration to new versions of the Windows operating system or adopt application virtualization technologies such as XenApp or App-V.

 AppDNA is a standalone product, but it's now included in the XenApp 7.5 Platinum license.

AppDNA includes preconfigured scenarios. For example, you can analyze the compatibility of your applications in case of the adoption of XenDesktop.

# System requirements

AppDNA is a client-server application. The server part is supported on Windows Server 2008 SP2 or later and on Windows 7 or later. In a production environment, Citrix recommends the use of server operating systems.

The client part is supported on all the server platforms, and it is also supported on Windows XP and Windows Vista.

 An AppDNA server cannot be installed on the same server where Citrix Licensing is already installed.

AppDNA requires Microsoft .NET Framework 3.5 SP1 and .NET Framework 4.0.

A Microsoft SQL Server database is required; you can use the Express version of SQLServer 2008 R2 or 2012 (remember, they have a built-in 10-GB database size limit).

# Usage

Working with AppDNA is simple. The basic workflow requires three steps, which are explained in the following sections.

## Import

First, you need to import your applications in AppDNA. When you import an application, AppDNA interrogates application files, registry entries, and API usage, and loads them into a SQL Server database.

You can import desktop applications directly in AppDNA if you have a Windows installer (`.msi`) or App-V (`.sft` or `.appv`) package. If not, you can use Install Capture, a feature that uses a virtual machine to capture the details of an application's installation.

For web applications, you can capture the web source files into an MSI file or, alternatively, you can use the AppDNA Directed Spider to crawl over the HTML pages, as shown in the following screenshot:

Importing a .msi file

## Analyze

When you start the analysis process, you select the reports that correspond to the platforms against which you want to test your applications. Analysis is a process that combines the information AppDNA has about the application, analyzes it against the selected target technologies, and generates the reports.

# Report

At the end of the analysis step, you can view a set of report views that provide the information that you need to plan, fix, and test your application portfolio.

The **Application Issues** and **Application Actions** views provide high-level overviews about the state of individual applications.

The **Remediation Issues** and **Remediation Actions** views provide detailed information about how to fix individual applications.

The **EstateView** report provides a consolidated overview of the state of the entire application portfolio. **Effort Calculator** can be useful to estimate the time, cost, and effort associated with the scenario you're evaluating. The following screenshot shows an example of application issues:

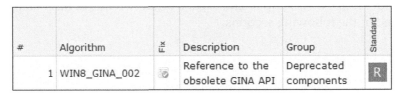

| # | Algorithm | Fix | Description | Group | Standard |
|---|-----------|-----|-------------|-------|----------|
| 1 | WIN8_GINA_002 | 🖫 | Reference to the obsolete GINA API | Deprecated components | R |

Reviewing application issues

# Summary

The logon process is the most hidden but important step when a user requests an application. Since it's not visible to the user, it should take the least possible time. A good knowledge of what's happening during the process and which components are involved can help to optimize it and solve typical issues.

With the help of some advanced features such as Session Reliability and workspace control, you can provide a good user experience, even during connectivity interruptions, or when moving from one device to another.

A common myth is that desktop and application virtualization technologies are only good for office applications. With some optimizations, tuning, and leveraging technologies provided by Citrix HDX, you can offer a high-definition user experience to your XenApp users, even if they are using mobile devices or mobile networks.

With HDX Monitor, you can check whether all the features are running and inspect all problems. With AppDNA, you can verify whether your applications are compatible with different operating systems and scenarios.

In the next chapter, you'll learn how to optimize your infrastructure for remote users and how to test the user experience using an open source network simulator, WANem.

# 4
# Publishing Applications through WAN Links

If you're administering a XenApp infrastructure for a while, someone has probably already asked you to give access to published applications for users who are not connected to your local LAN. The external access could be for teleworkers, branch offices, or outsourcers that even work in a different continent.

The **Independent Computing Architecture (ICA)** protocol is known for its excellent performance over slow links and its low bandwidth usage. In this chapter, you'll learn the following topics:

- Differences between LAN and WAN links
- Specific optimizations available in XenApp for WAN links
- How to test your farm's behavior over WAN links before going to production
- How to monitor network connections
- Solutions that Citrix offers to optimize and accelerate WAN connections

## Characteristics of a WAN link

The most general definition of a **Wide Area Network (WAN)** is a network that covers a broad area using public or private network transports. In this chapter, we're going to analyze the scenario of a remote user who needs to access an application published by a XenApp infrastructure located in your data center.

The connection between the user and your infrastructure might be on a private link (usually a leased line) or on a public network (usually the Internet). The most important parameters of a link are as follows:

- The available bandwidth
- The latency
- The reliability

A common belief is that bandwidth is the main problem in remote connections; this is usually false. Fast access to the Internet is now available in most countries, and mobile operators can also offer high-speed connections (3G, 4G, and so on). Dedicated links can be leased with guaranteed bandwidth, and with technologies such as **Multiprotocol Label Switching (MPLS)**, carriers now offer geographic links with high speed.

The latency, on the contrary, depends on the distance between the two endpoints of a link and the transmission medium; it's usually a fixed value.

For example, let's consider a satellite link. Geosynchronous satellites orbit at about 42 km from the Earth; radio signals take about 250 ms to reach them, so this type of link introduces a fixed delay of 500 ms, as shown in the following diagram:

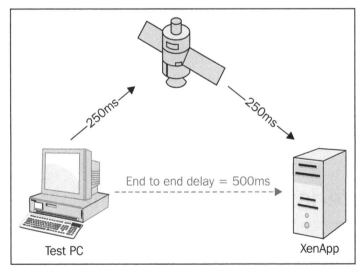

Latency in a satellite link

A high value of latency is very problematic, especially with graphical applications. Later in this chapter, you'll learn some advanced features of XenApp; you can use them to minimize the impact of the latency on the user experience.

# Emulating links with WANem

If you're planning to publish applications on geographic links, it's very important to test how these applications perform. You'll learn later in this chapter how the optimizations work to improve the user experience.

Plan a complete **User Acceptance Test (UAT)** phase before going to production, if possible, with real users. In this section, you'll learn how to use an open source tool, WANem, to emulate a WAN link.

I usually prepare some test scenarios and ask users to give a score from 1 (bad) to 5 (good) for the user experience. The following table is an example of the feedback I got from a test session. It includes varying bandwidth (columns) and latency (rows), and is without any optimizations:

| Time | 100 KB/s | 200 KB/s | 300 KB/s | 500 KB/s |
| --- | --- | --- | --- | --- |
| 10 ms | 2 | 3 | 4 | 5 |
| 50 ms | 2 | 2 | 3 | 4 |
| 150 ms | 1 | 1 | 1 | 2 |

# Installing

WANem is distributed as a bootable CD, based on Linux Knoppix. The operating system runs live from the CD, that is, you don't need to install it on the machine's hard disk.

WANem does not require many resources; any i386 PC or (virtual) server with at least 1 GB RAM will be OK. The administrative interface is web-based, so you can configure WANem from any device with a web browser.

The ISO image is downloadable from the official website: `http://wanem.sourceforge.net`.

During the boot process, you'll be asked for network parameters; WANem supports both DHCP and manual configuration, as shown in the following screenshot:

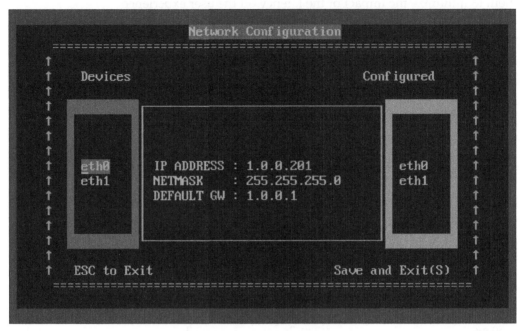

The WANem network configuration

At the end of the boot process, you're presented with a command prompt. WANem is now ready, and you can connect to its web interface, `http://WANemIP/WANem`.

# Configuring

In order to be able to emulate a WAN link, you have to force the packets between a test client and your XenApp server to flow via WANem. The simplest and best way is to place all three devices on the same network and configure static routes on the PC and server, as shown in the following diagram:

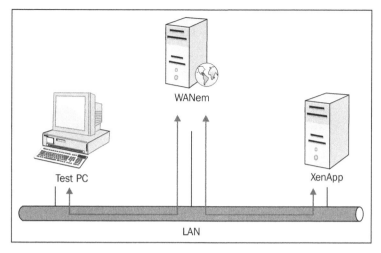

Packet routing required for WANem

Let's assume the following IP addresses:

- Test PC (XA-CLIENT01): 1.0.0.200
- XenApp Server (XA-APP01): 1.0.0.20
- WANem virtual appliance (XA-WANEM): 1.0.0.201

In the client, you have to configure a static route to send the packets destined for the server through the WANem appliance, as shown in the following command:

```
C:\>route add 1.0.0.20 mask 255.255.255.255 1.0.0.201
```

On the other hand, on the server, you have to configure a static route for the returning traffic (from the server to the client), as shown in the following command:

```
C:\>route add 1.0.0.200 mask 255.255.255.255 1.0.0.201
```

To check whether the routing is working, start an infinite `ping` command from the client to the server, as shown in the following command:

```
C:\>ping -t 1.0.0.20
```

You should see the replies coming from the server in a few milliseconds.

Now, connect to the WANem web interface, choose **Basic Mode**, insert a delay time of 100 ms, and click on **Apply settings**, as shown in the following screenshot:

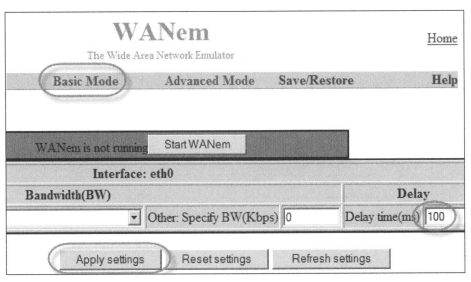

Changing the delay time

If the configuration is OK, you should now see the replies to the ping command coming with about 200 ms of delay, as shown in the following screenshot:

```
Reply from 1.0.0.20: bytes=32 time<1ms TTL=127
Reply from 1.0.0.20: bytes=32 time<1ms TTL=127
Reply from 1.0.0.20: bytes=32 time<1ms TTL=127
Reply from 1.0.0.20: bytes=32 time<1ms TTL=127
Reply from 1.0.0.20: bytes=32 time<1ms TTL=127
Reply from 1.0.0.20: bytes=32 time<1ms TTL=127
Reply from 1.0.0.20: bytes=32 time=204ms TTL=127
Reply from 1.0.0.20: bytes=32 time=203ms TTL=127
Reply from 1.0.0.20: bytes=32 time=205ms TTL=127
```

Differences in reply time with WANem enabled

# Using

Through WANem web interface, you can change the settings of the emulated link.

In **Basic Mode**, you can set the bandwidth (choosing from standard values or entering custom ones) and delay (the latency). Only one rule is possible for each network interface.

The emulated link is symmetrical; that's why in the previous example, if you set a delay of 100 ms, the **Round Trip Time (RTT)** measured by the `ping` command is 200 ms.

In **Advanced Mode**, you can add different rules based on the source and destination addresses.

For each rule, you can define specific network characteristics as follows:

- **Packet limit**: This is the maximum number of packets WANem can keep in the forwarding queue. If the queue is full, the new packets are discarded.

- **Symmetrical network**: If this is set to `Yes`, the rule will be applied in both directions; if set to `No`, the rule will be applied only for the packets that come from the specified source address.

- **Delay**: This is the latency of the link. You can specify a static value, add a random jitter, or choose from one of the statistic distributions. The supported delay resolution is 10 ms, so use multiples of this value.

- **Loss**: This is the percentage of packets that will be randomly dropped. With the optional correlation value, you can emulate packet burst losses.

- **Duplication**: This is the percentage of packets that will be randomly duplicated. With the optional correlation value, you can emulate packet burst duplications.

- **Corruption**: This is the percentage of packets that will be randomly corrupted. WANem introduces a single-bit error at a random offset in the packet.

- **Reordering**: This is the percentage of packets that will be forwarded out of the sequence.

- **Bandwidth**: This is the available bandwidth. For good accuracy, don't go lower than 120 KB/s.

- **Disconnection**: This is used to simulate an unreliable network. You can choose how WANem emulates disconnections (TCP resets, ICMP messages, and so on) and the **Mean Time To Failure (MTTF)** and **Mean Time To Recovery (MTTR)** values for random disconnections.

# WANalyzer

WANem can also be used to analyze a WAN link. WANalyzer is able to measure the following network characteristics of the connection to a target host:

- Latency
- Loss of packets
- Jitter
- Available bandwidth

The following screenshot displays these characteristics:

| RESULTS | |
|---|---|
| Remote host IP | 1.0.0.20 |
| Time of measurement | 13:54:28 |
| Latency | 89.96 ms |
| Loss of packet | 0 % |
| Jitter | 89.9602 |
| Available Band Width | 1.29752 Mbps |

The WANalyzer result

# Optimizing the ICA® protocol

The ICA protocol is a proprietary protocol designed by Citrix and is used for client/server communication in XenApp and XenDesktop. It runs over TCP port 1494, but it may be encapsulated in **Common Gateway Protocol** (**CGP**) over TCP port 2598 when using Session Reliability (recommended with XenApp 7.5, as stated in the *Chapter 3, Monitor and Optimize End User Experience*). You'll learn the importance of CGP later in this chapter.

# ICA® virtual channels

The ICA protocol comprises virtual channels, as shown in the following diagram. A virtual channel consists of a driver running on the client side; it communicates with a server-side application. It transports data for redirected peripherals (keyboard, printer, and so on) or for Citrix functionalities (clipboard, licensing, and so on). A couple of channels are also available for **Original Equipment Manufacturers (OEMs)**.

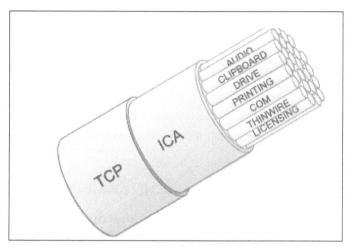

Virtual Channels in the ICA protocol

# Virtual channel priorities

The ICA protocol implements an internal **Quality of Service (QoS)**, assigning different priorities to different virtual channel groups.

The protocol defines the following four priorities:

- 0 = very high
- 1 = high
- 2 = medium
- 3 = low

You can change the priority assigned to a virtual channel with the `VirtualChannels` value in the registry key located at `HKLM\System\CurrentControlSet\Control\ Terminal Server\Wds\icawd\MultiStreamIca\`, as shown in the following screenshot:

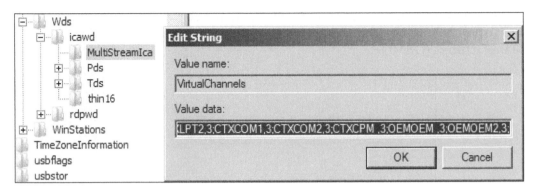

Changing the virtual channels' priority

The format of the registry string value is as follows:

- CHANNELNAME,PRIORITY; CHANNELNAME,PRIORITY;...

The list of the different virtual channels and their description is included in the Citrix knowledge base at `http://support.citrix.com/article/CTX131001`.

# ICA® MultiStream

With the use of virtual channels' priority, you can implement a QoS within a single ICA connection. Network devices have no visibility of the different virtual channels, so you can't give priority to a specific channel with network-based QoS. For example, if you're experiencing poor audio quality due to network congestion caused by both ICA and non-ICA traffic, network administrators can only prioritize the entire ICA session.

XenApp 7.5 includes a feature named ICA MultiStream; it configures the ICA protocol to use different TCP connections for the classes of a service. Each TCP connection binds to a different TCP port on the server, and network administrators can apply different QoS classes to the different connections. ICA MultiStream requires Session Reliability to be enabled.

If you're using Citrix CloudBridge (covered later in this chapter), you do not need to enable ICA MultiStream; CloudBridge natively optimizes the different ICA streams.

The following diagram displays the differences between normal mode and MultiStream:

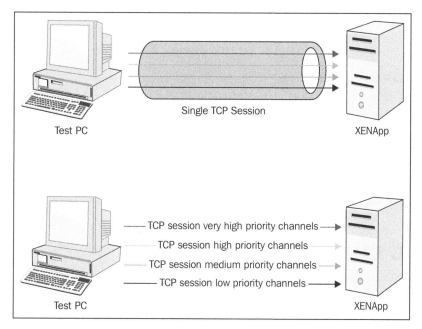

Differences between normal mode and MultiStream

# Enabling ICA® MultiStream

ICA MultiStream is controlled by Citrix policies.

First, you need to enable it at the server level with a computer policy, `ICA\Multi-Stream Connections\Multi-Stream computer setting = Enabled`.

When configuring this setting, reboot the server to ensure that the changes take effect.

Then, with the Multi-Port policy, you can define up to four different TCP ports and assign them to the different priorities.

Make sure that the chosen ports are not already used by other services on your XenApp servers. With the `netstat -na` command, you can list the ports in the Listening state.

Finally, enable the **Multi-Stream** user setting with a user policy; by default, indeed, it's disabled for all users.

For more details about ICA MultiStream, refer to `http://blogs.citrix.com/2011/08/25/enhanced-qos-via-multi-stream-ica/`.

## Audio over UDP

In *Chapter 3, Monitor and Optimize End User Experience*, I covered the Audio redirection feature and the ability to use the UDP protocol to transport audio stream. Two settings for this feature are also included in the **Multi-Stream Connections** category as follows:

- **Audio over UDP**: This enables/disables the UDP ports on the server
- **Audio UDP port range**: This configures the port range that the VDA can use to allocate a UDP port pair to exchange audio packet data with the client

# Traffic shaping

In some scenarios, it is very important to limit the maximum bandwidth used by different sessions. Even if you're using a high-speed link, shaping some streams is a good practice. Consider, for example, a user working with a scanner; when the scanner sends the image to the application that runs on the XenApp server, it can easily saturate the available bandwidth.

XenApp offers a category of user settings to limit the bandwidth used by the different supported redirections, as shown in the following screenshot:

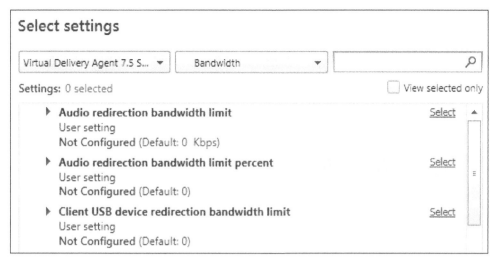

Bandwidth policy settings

You can limit the overall session bandwidth and/or the bandwidth used for the following:

- Audio redirection
- Client USB device redirection
- Clipboard redirection
- COM port redirection
- File redirection
- HDX MediaStream redirection
- LPT port redirection
- Printer redirection
- TWAIN device redirection

You can define a fixed limit value (in KB per second) and a percentage of the total session bandwidth; you can also completely turn off a channel if it is unused. If you configure both the settings, the most restrictive one is applied.

 A configured bandwidth limit is always enforced, even when no other channels are in use.

# Monitoring bandwidth usage

In *Chapter 2, Monitor and Optimize Infrastructure – Director and EdgeSight®*, you learned that Citrix EdgeSight, now integrated in Director, provides two key features:

- Performance Management
- Network Analysis

The Network Analysis feature gives a very detailed view of network connections, as shown in the following screenshot:

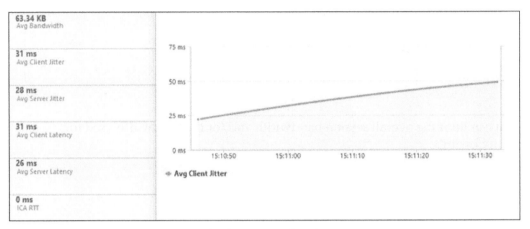

Network information in Citrix Director

# Configuring

Citrix EdgeSight requires the deployment of a virtual appliance, NetScaler Insight Center, to monitor, capture, and analyze data. The virtual appliance is available in the download area of the Citrix website; remember that you need a valid NetScaler Enterprise or Platinum license to download it and activate the Network Analysis feature.

Insight can collect two types of data: Web Insight data (for web applications bound to a NetScaler appliance) and HDX Insight data (for XenApp and XenDesktop connections).

After having installed and configured the Insight appliance, you have to configure your NetScaler appliance to send data to it. If users access the NetScaler appliances through a VPN (single-hop mode), the Insight appliance will configure NetScaler automatically; if, instead, NetScaler is in transparent mode, you have to add NetScaler Insight Center as an AppFlow collector on each NetScaler appliance.

The configuration must be performed using the command-line interface; refer to the NetScaler documentation for more details:

```
http://support.citrix.com/proddocs/topic/ni-10-5-map/
ni-enable-hdx-wrapper-con.html
```

## Network latency versus ICA® RTT

One of most important types of data available in the **Network Analysis** pane is the ICA RTT. This value is slightly different from the network latency in the following ways:

- Network latency is the time interval measured between the ICA client device and the XenApp server, independent of processing time.

- The ICA round trip is the time interval measured at the client between the first step (user action) and the last step (the graphical response is displayed). It can be thought of as a measurement of the *screen lag* that a user experiences.

A category of policy settings (**End User Monitoring**) is available to enable/disable the calculation of ICA RTT, configure the frequency at which calculations are performed, and determine whether calculations are also performed for idle connections.

# Receiver™ for HTML5

Receiver for HTML5 offers users access to virtual desktops and apps provided by XenDesktop and XenApp, using only a standard web browser. It's bundled with StoreFront and does not require a separate installation on the user's device.

The latest versions of Receiver for HTML5 support the use of WebSockets, a technology that allows a full-duplex communication using only a single TCP socket. The use of WebSockets can optimize the network bandwidth usage, thus reducing the overhead required to open multiple HTTP connections between the browser and StoreFront server.

By default, WebSocket connections are prohibited; three policy settings are available to configure this feature:

- **WebSockets connections**: This is used to enable/disable WebSockets
- **WebSockets port number**: This is used to configure the port for incoming connections (by default, 8008)
- **WebSockets trusted origin server list**: This is used to define a list of trusted origin servers; only connections that originate from one of these addresses are accepted by the server

The following screenshot shows the three policy settings that are available:

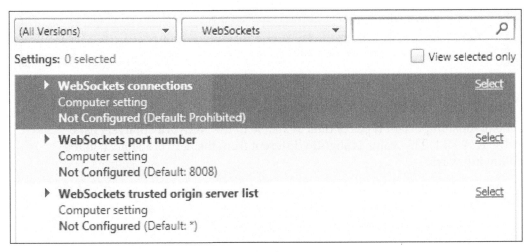

Configuring WebSockets connections

# CloudBridge™

CloudBridge (formerly, Branch Repeater) is the Citrix solution to optimize WAN connections. It's a family of WAN accelerators, which are explained as follows:

- Repeater appliances that are designed for use in data centers
- CloudBridge appliances that are designed for use in branch offices
- Software plugins that are run on Windows laptops and workstations

Some CloudBridge appliances are shipped with a licensed version of Microsoft Windows Server 2012 R2 Standard Edition that runs on a virtual machine within the appliance.

A virtual appliance, CloudBridge VPX, is also available, and it can be hosted on Citrix XenServer, VMware ESX or ESXi, Microsoft Hyper-V, and **Amazon Web Services (AWS)** virtualization platforms.

# Licensed bandwidth

When selecting the correct appliance for your infrastructure, the most important factor is that it supports your WAN link. If your site has multiple links that are to be accelerated by a single appliance, the appliance should support the total speed of all the WAN links.

The maximum supported speed is determined by a combination of the appliance hardware and product license. The licensed bandwidth limit is the maximum link speed that is supported by the license.

# Deployment

For sites with one WAN link, the suggested deployment mode is inline, as shown in the following diagram:

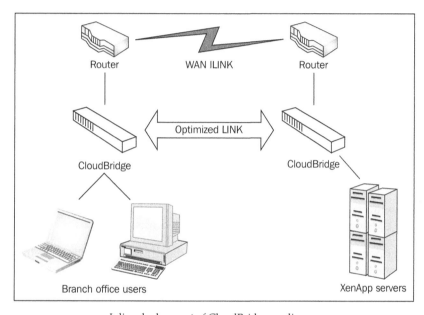

Inline deployment of CloudBridge appliances

The appliance uses two bridged Ethernet ports for the inline mode; packets enter one Ethernet port and exit through the other.

Inline mode has the following advantages:

- It's completely transparent for the rest of the network
- It does not require any reconfiguration of your network equipment
- It gives the maximum performance
- It's very easy to deploy and configure

# Features

CloudBridge is a complete solution to accelerate applications and services accessed through a WAN link. In addition to the ICA protocol, it can natively accelerate, without further configuration, Windows file sharing (CIFS), Outlook/Exchange (MAPI), HTTP, and HTTPS.

Local caching, deduplication, and compression can dramatically reduce the amount of data sent on the link, thus improving the end user experience on slow links.

The availability of a software-based network accelerator, the CloudBridge Plug-in, makes it possible to give mobile users the same benefits without the need of a CloudBridge appliance, which is still recommended for branch offices.

# Summary

A common request from users is to access their applications outside the company, using different types of connections. The ICA protocol used by XenApp is designed to also work with low-speed, high-latency connections; system administrators can also use some advanced features to improve the user experience.

Citrix offers a family of network accelerators, CloudBridge, which can be used to optimize the connections through WAN or mobile links.

WANem, an open source tool, is helpful to simulate how applications behave with different connections. With the deployment of NetScaler Insight, network data is available in Citrix Director.

# Index

## U

**UnassignedCount attribute, Get-BrokerCatalog cmdlet** 39
**unique identifier (UUID)** 26
**universal printer driver**
  versus native printer driver 75
**Universal Print Server**
  about 74
  using 74
**UsedCount attribute, Get-BrokerCatalog cmdlet** 39
**User Acceptance Test (UAT)** 83
**user experience, improving with Citrix® HDX™**
  about 75
  HDX™ MediaStream 75
  HDX™ Mobile 77
  HDX™ Monitor 78
**user layer, FMA** 7
**user sessions, maintaining**
  automatic client reconnection 73
  ICA® Keep-Alive feature 73
  Session Reliability 72
  workspace control 74
  XenApp®, missing features 74

## V

**Virtual Delivery Agent (VDA)** 26
**virtual infrastructure**
  connecting, to MCS 24, 25
**virtual infrastructure, Citrix® Director**
  monitoring 46-48
**VM-hosted apps, resource layer** 11
**Voice over IP (VoIP)** 77

## W

**WANalyzer**
  network characteristics, measuring 88
**WANem**
  configuring 84-86
  installing 83
  network characteristics, defining 87
  URL 83
  used, for emulating WAN link 83

  using 86
  WANalyzer 88
**WAN link**
  about 81, 82
  emulating, with WANem 83
  example 82
  parameters 82
**Wide Area Network link.** *See* **WAN link**
**Windows Dynamic Fair Share Scheduling (Windows DFSS)** 50, 51
**Windows Media redirection, HDX™ MediaStream** 76
**Windows System Resource Manager (WSRM)** 51
**worker servers** 5
**workspace control, user sessions** 74

## X

**XenApp®**
  issue 61
**XenApp® 6.0**
  versus XenApp® 7.5 30
**XenApp® 7.5**
  versus XenApp® 6.0 30
**XenApp® installation size, expanding**
  Divide option 16
  Scale out option 17
  Scale up option 16
**XenApp® installations, monitoring with Microsoft PowerShell**
  about 37
  Get-BrokerApplicationInstance cmdlet, using 40
  Get-BrokerCatalog cmdlet, using 39
  Get-BrokerController cmdlet, using 39
  Get-BrokerMachine cmdlet, using 37, 38
  objects, counting 40, 41
**XenApp® site**
  StoreFront configuration 58
  versus zone 58
**XML Service**
  about 36
  Average Transaction Time 36
  Concurrent Transactions 36
  Transactions/sec 36

**Thank you for buying**

# Citrix® XenApp® 7.x Performance Essentials

# About Packt Publishing

Packt, pronounced 'packed', published its first book "Mastering phpMyAdmin for Effective MySQL Management" in April 2004 and subsequently continued to specialize in publishing highly focused books on specific technologies and solutions.

Our books and publications share the experiences of your fellow IT professionals in adapting and customizing today's systems, applications, and frameworks. Our solution based books give you the knowledge and power to customize the software and technologies you're using to get the job done. Packt books are more specific and less general than the IT books you have seen in the past. Our unique business model allows us to bring you more focused information, giving you more of what you need to know, and less of what you don't.

Packt is a modern, yet unique publishing company, which focuses on producing quality, cutting-edge books for communities of developers, administrators, and newbies alike. For more information, please visit our website: www.packtpub.com.

# About Packt Enterprise

In 2010, Packt launched two new brands, Packt Enterprise and Packt Open Source, in order to continue its focus on specialization. This book is part of the Packt Enterprise brand, home to books published on enterprise software – software created by major vendors, including (but not limited to) IBM, Microsoft and Oracle, often for use in other corporations. Its titles will offer information relevant to a range of users of this software, including administrators, developers, architects, and end users.

# Writing for Packt

We welcome all inquiries from people who are interested in authoring. Book proposals should be sent to author@packtpub.com. If your book idea is still at an early stage and you would like to discuss it first before writing a formal book proposal, contact us; one of our commissioning editors will get in touch with you.

We're not just looking for published authors; if you have strong technical skills but no writing experience, our experienced editors can help you develop a writing career, or simply get some additional reward for your expertise.

**Getting Started with Citrix® CloudPortal™**

ISBN: 978-1-78217-682-4 Paperback: 128 pages

Get acquainted with Citrix Systems®' CPSM and CPBM in order to administer cloud services smoothly and comprehensively

1. Overview of CPSM and CPBM architectures, and planning CPSM and CPBM.

2. Become efficient in product management, workflow management, and billing and pricing management.

3. Provision services efficiently to cloud consumers and clients.

**Getting Started with Citrix VDI-in-a-Box**

ISBN: 978-1-78217-104-1 Paperback: 86 pages

Design and deploy virtual desktops using Citrix VDI-in-a-Box

1. Design a Citrix VDI-in-a-Box solution.

2. Get the budget for Citrix VDI-in-a-Box by building a case.

3. Implement a Citrix VDI-in-a-Box proof of concept and Citrix VDI-in-a-Box solution.

Please check **www.PacktPub.com** for information on our titles

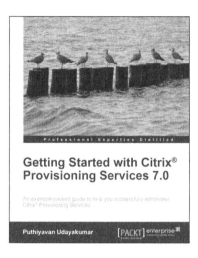

**Getting Started with Citrix®
Provisioning Services 7.0**

**Getting Started with Citrix®
Provisioning Services 7.0**

ISBN: 978-1-78217-670-1          Paperback: 134 pages

An example-packed guide to help you successfully
administer Citrix® Provisioning Services

1. Install and configure Citrix Provisioning
   Services quickly and efficiently.

2. Master the architecture of Citrix Provisioning
   Services.

3. Successfully manage and operate Citrix
   Provisioning Services.

Puthiyavan Udayakumar

**Citrix® XenDesktop® 7 Cookbook**

ISBN: 978-1-78217-746-3          Paperback: 410 pages

Over 35 recipes to help you implement a fully
featured XenDesktop® 7 architecture with a rich
and powerful VDI experience

1. Implement the XenDesktop 7 architecture and
   its satellite components.

2. Learn how to publish desktops and
   applications to the end user devices, optimizing
   their performance and increasing the general
   security.

3. Designed in a manner which will allow you to
   progress gradually from one chapter to another
   or to implement a single component only
   referring to the specific topic.

Gaspare A. Silvestri

Please check **www.PacktPub.com** for information on our titles

Lightning Source UK Ltd.
Milton Keynes UK
UKOW07f2207290515

252597UK00003B/55/P